11/2020

SPIRIT WINDOWS

SPIRIT WINDOWS

A Handbook of Spiritual Growth Resources for Leaders of

- Retreats
- Prayer Groups
- Lenten Series
- Contemplative Prayer Settings
- Church School Classes
- Meditation Groups
- Bible Study Groups
- Women's Events
- Church Officer Events
- Days of Reflections

Ann Z. Kulp

Bridge Resources
Louisville, Kentucky

Edited by Beth Basham
Book and cover design by Peggy Claire Calhoun
Cover illustration by Michael Podesta

First edition

Published by Bridge Resources
Louisville, Kentucky

Web site address: http://www.bridgeresources.org

PRINTED IN THE UNITED STATES OF AMERICA

98 99 00 01 02 03 04 05 06 07 — 10 9 8 7 6 5 4 3 2 1

Library of Congress Cataloging-in-Publication Data

Kulp, Ann Z., date.
    Spirit windows : a handbook of spiritual growth resources for leaders Ann Z. Kulp.
    p.   cm.
  Includes bibliographical references.
  ISBN 1-57895-021-X
  1. Spiritual life—Christianity. 2. Spiritual formation. 3. Small groups—Religious aspects.
  I. Title.
BV4501.2.K793   1998
248—dc21   97-43927

A window, or "wind eye,"
was originally a hole in the wall
that opened the darkness
to the holy power of light.
Some ancient communities
worshiped the first ray of light
to reach a window.

—Ann Wall Frank*

*Reprinted from *Bless This House:
A Collection of Blessings to Make Your House
Your Home*, p. 101. Copyright © 1996 by
Ann Wall Frank. Used with permission by
NTC/Contemporary Publishing Company,
Chicago, IL.

Dedication . . .

This work probably would never have come to
fruition had it not been for my introduction to the
Shalem Institute for Spiritual Formation in the
Washington, D.C. area. Through their numerous
programs, I was introduced to fresh new ways to
express my yearning for God. It is out of those
experiences that much of the content in this book
is derived, both explicit and implicit. I am
indebted and grateful to the company of saints at
Shalem who have passed on to me the importance
of attentive silence in waiting on God.

With Gratitude and Appreciation . . .

To my parents, Ethel and David Zimmerman, who introduced me to the church community from age three, and whose example of faith and commitment inspired me to pursue my own spiritual journey.

To Paul, who helped me get started—literally—and who was a steady support, gofer, and ministering companion amid the pressures of deadlines and multiple commitments.

To Karen, who enthusiastically entered into the original project with the creative suggestion of replacing the star in the windowpane with an appropriate symbol for each section divider.

To David, mastermind of the computer, who encouraged, assisted, and came to the rescue, even from a long distance.

To Rosalind Ekermeyer, who shared in this project in its infant stages, offering her loving presence and caring assistance at retreats and being willing to spend hours helping to proofread the original edition before a publisher ever laid eyes on it.

To Beth Basham, an enthusiastic and encouraging editor, whose words "Reframe your mind/spirit, woman!" will always be delightfully remembered whenever I pass through other valleys of despair.

To Michael Podesta, friend of twenty years, whose inspired talent to create exquisite graphic designs with words is matched only by the depth of his spirit.

To the Graduate Theological Foundation, without whose requirement for a Doctor of Ministry project this piece would never have taken form.

To all those who have participated in any event I have led, adding to my understanding and appreciation of the Spirit's work, despite anything I may have to offer.

Contents

Introduction 1

When the well is running dry, where do I turn?

Daily our psyche is bombarded by stimuli that command a response on either the conscious or the subconscious level. We have been catapulted since the midcentury into a schizophrenic kind of existence with an ever-increasing emphasis on speed, performance, multiple roles, and global proximity. Our spiritual gyroscope, which serves to maintain the core of our being in a constant relationship with God, is under persistent attack. It is not so simple to lead a simple life. The human spirit feels this tension and is torn between the alternatives that are offered to keep the well from running dry.

As a result, there seems to be a perennial request among the churched, as well as the unchurched, for those things that nurture the spirit. These "things" go by different names and sometimes cannot be identified by any name at all. They are simply indescribable feelings. What they share

in common might be termed "an experience of the holy."

The assumption within the organized church has been that spiritual growth will take place within the context of inspired preaching, meaningful worship, moving music, stimulating Christian educational programs, and a relevant mission focus. Some churches may emphasize using personal daily devotional materials. These traditional forms are helpful but seem to fall short. The deeper hunger is still apparent. One hardly knows how to express the felt need, and those listening scarcely know how to respond.

This handbook addresses the necessity for resources in the realm of spiritual enrichment—whether it be a church school class learning about the different types of prayer, a Lenten series reflecting on Scripture, a one-day retreat for church leaders, or a weekend retreat for "re-treating" ourselves. This collection is intended to give one a choice of materials that can be

assembled to suit particular needs. While numerous devotional and worship publications are available, there seems to be a dearth of spiritual enrichment resources. It is hoped that this resource will offer some new approaches as it pulls together some familiar themes. May it spur you on to create new ones of your own.

Personal Statement

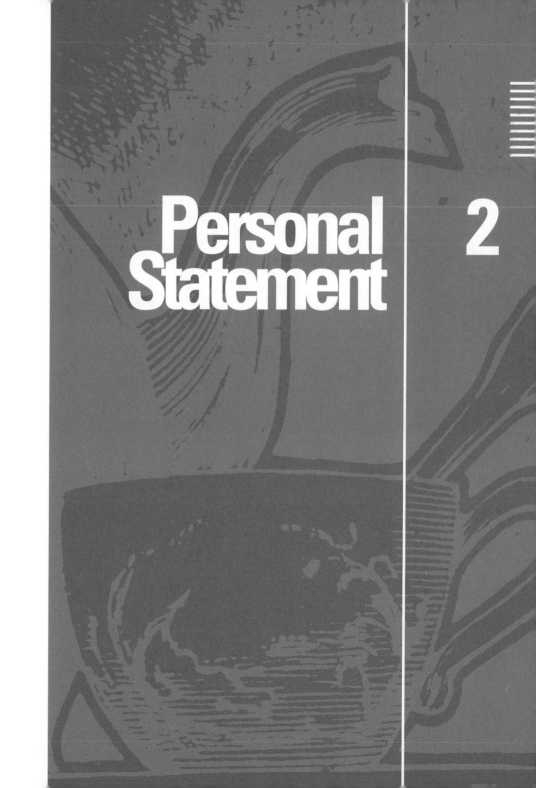

2

▌ Intent

Spirit Windows is not written out of any success pattern that I offer as a panacea for spiritual need or hunger. It is written from the same sense of frustration that each of us experiences with the demands of life—those things that crowd out the time we crave to spend on our personal spiritual nurture.

I, too, struggle to find the time, the way, the space, or even the desire to be with God. I acknowledge the secret nudgings that lie behind my busy schedule and overcommitted lifestyle. And yet I know that basically I do what I choose to do, despite all the excuses I may offer as legitimate for neglecting daily time with God. Worse yet is when I find myself advocating and suggesting ways for others to spend time with God but do not abide by my own recommendations! I seem to be playing God while shutting God out. Those who work in the organized church are especially vulnerable. This is a sensitive area, because none of us feel that we offer enough of ourselves to God in the open, free, and selfless way that we would like.

As a result of these personal discoveries, struggles, and joys, I am convinced that others, too, would appreciate new or fresh ways of being open to God's presence. In our yearning for the divine Presence, we are reminded that the same Presence also yearns for us.

▌ Intent

Because I believe that spiritual-growth events are intended to help us focus on our relationship with God, the resources in Spirit Windows are meant to assist in opening us to the deeper places within, where the "still small voice" awaits our attention. The ideas and samples that are offered here are only a few of the many entrances or "windows" into God's presence. All these will be centered on the Word. All are intended to help us set aside

- our compulsion of intellect that grasps for comprehension
- our curiosity that desires a particular insight and
- our control of circumstances that wishes to predict an outcome.

We will instead try to

- let go of any expectation
- accept the simplest of directions
- rest with the suggestions, not judging them
- experience silence in the midst of sound
- record impressions as well as feelings, noting resistance but not evaluating
- thank God for being present, however that presence touches or doesn't touch us
- persevere again the next day, trusting in God, not ourselves
- be open for the kind of knowledge that comes from the spiritual heart.

Most of the experiences that are presented here are repeatable in one's own daily time. Some practices may open our desire and receptivity to God more readily than others. At different times in our lives we may find ourselves preferring different approaches, which may include an approach of simple presence with no particular method. The important aspect is being willing to be open to God—however that may take place.

Assumptions 3

- ▌ **About Human Nature**

- ▌ **About God**

The following assumptions helped to ground the writing of this book.

▌ About Human Nature

- Within the organized church, most people seek ways to be spiritually nurtured.
- Despite our best intentions, most of us do not take the time to be with God through personal spiritual disciplines.
- We are easily caught up in the value of society, which caters to the importance of intellectual activities and the accumulation of knowledge.
- We are not clear about the difference between *knowledge about* God as opposed to *knowing* God or *being present* to God—one being focused on the head, the other on the heart.
- An environment of openness and acceptance will help to reduce any fear and resistance that might be present.

▌ About God

- We can be present with God in any place at any time.
- When we are open and listening in an attentive way, we create an atmosphere of willingness to be present with God.
- Opening to God's presence can take place through many paths. We do not all relate equally well to all paths. However, we need to take note of those paths that seem right while being willing to examine our resistance to those that cause us discomfort.
- Learning to discern what is of God and what is not of God is a primary goal, since it can help us with decision making in our daily lives.
- The Word is eternal—focused on God in creation, in Jesus Christ as the living example, and on the Holy Spirit who draws us toward our true nature in God and makes us aware of graced moments.

Expectations 4

■ **Of the Group**

■ **Of the Leader**

The following expectations helped to guide the development of this book.

These expectations should be presented at a beginning session, either verbally or as a handout.

▌ Of the Group

The group will be able to

- have the freedom to participate and not be worried about odds and ends, or being the leader's assistant
- relax
- feel free to share or not share without any pressure
- keep the confidence of each person during the time together
- be sensitive to others' contributions, accepting one another's experience for what it is without judgment
- be willing to share the allotted time with others, including speaking time.

▌ Of the Leader

The leader will be able to

- begin and end on time, unless the group agrees to change the schedule
- set the mood and expectation level (or lack of expectations); there should be no false hopes
- keep things moving, but not rushed
- plan, but plan loosely so adjustments in content and time may be made if needed
- listen carefully to group responses and adjust plans accordingly (be open to sacrificing the plan for something the group finds needful)
- renegotiate time if it is running short; the group may prefer to give up something else, even free time
- avoid getting drawn into the kinds of questions that invite discussion, indicating in advance that this is not a class, and offering to meet privately with individuals at another time.

Reminder: The ultimate leader of the group is God's Holy Spirit blowing through us. All we can do is to assist in the creation of an environment where others can become open to God's presence.

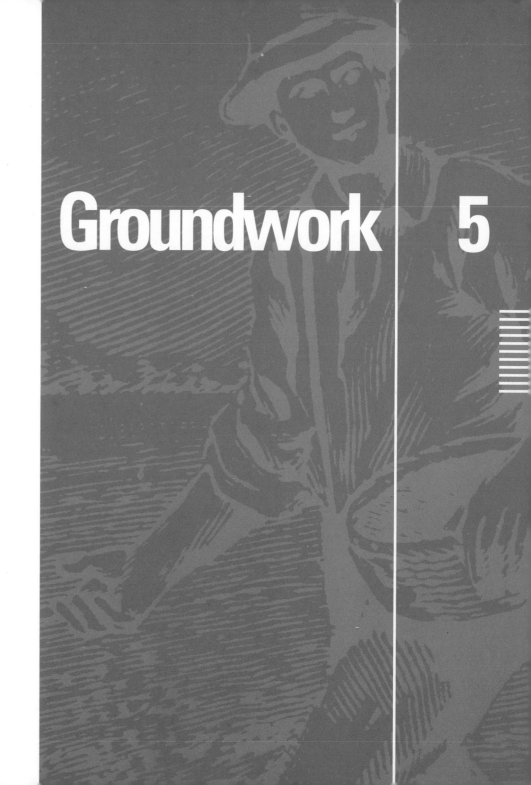

Groundwork 5

▌ The Nitty-Gritty

I have called this section "The Nitty-Gritty" because it is usually the part that causes the most problems, the part that precedes the event, and the part that pulls it all together. Because so much depends on what is done in advance, this section provides helpful guidelines for planning and organizing your event.

▌ Meeting with Those Involved

The first meeting, if planning for a big event, could be with a small leadership team. Discuss all the items found in this chapter, identifying who will be responsible for what. Ensure, if possible, that all necessary preparation is done in advance of the retreat so that everyone may enjoy participating without anxiety. It is also worthy to note that the more people involved in the advance preparation, the higher the level of investment and contagious enthusiasm.

▌ Establishing a Goal

Determining the nature of the event. For whom is this special time being planned? Is there a particular theme with which the group is already working? Is there a need that reminds them of a Scripture passage for a launching-off point? Is there a season of the year that speaks to a unique topic?

Reaching a consensus. At this first meeting, after an assortment of ideas has trickled in, seek discernment of the goal by engaging in silent prayer. Then share any images, symbols, words, phrases, pictures, or ideas that might have come to each person, accepting whatever

comes, even if nothing. Try to gain a consensus, while being open to any changes to the goal that may come at a later time.

▌ Selecting a Time

Choose a time that would best meet the purpose of the event.

- A morning, an afternoon, or an evening event (1–2 hours)
- A series of mornings or evenings (1–2 hours each)
- A one-day retreat or program (3–6 hours)
- An overnight or a weekend retreat

▌ Scheduling

In scheduling the different segments of an event, consideration should be given to

- having adequate space
- being flexible (one *does not* have to stick with the plan; the needs of the audience are more important than the plan)
- including time for silence as well as free time
- changing the pace, especially if there is a large block of time
- varying the group size (total gathering, small groups, individual time).

▌Assigning Responsibilities

The following considerations are part of the critical mass of detail work that go into making events successful. If one person is responsible for meeting all these needs, or even most of them, there will be less enthusiasm and investment and an increased probability of burnout. Each item needs to be addressed carefully, not as an afterthought. Participants can sense the importance that the leaders have attached to these seemingly more minor things. Yet they can be critical to the success of the event.

1. Environment

This important area of providing the right environment is probably one most often neglected. If people are not comfortable or if the setting does not invite openness and relaxation, the event cannot reach its maximum potential. Hard, cold chairs, classroom-type setups, and overhead fluorescent lighting are among the worst offenders. Consider the following suggestions for creating an environment that will allow participants to engage in spiritual reflection.

Seating

Preferably, people should be seated in a circle or semicircle to facilitate greater group intimacy. Rows of chairs lead to a formal setting, which is not inviting for a spirituality event. If the group is too large for this arrangement, several rows can be placed in a semicircle. People need to be able to see one another. Folding metal chairs should be a last resort. Comfortable chairs assist participants in their attentiveness. If comfortable chairs are not available, and if the group is willing, floor cushions can be used instead, especially for small groups.

Floor

While it is not always possible, it is highly desirable to meet in a room with a rug or carpet. It connotes warmth, both physically and environmentally. A rug absorbs sound and assists with the silent moments. It often suggests homeyness.

Lighting

Although this may necessitate a little extra effort, soft lighting is desirable. This can be in the form of floor or table lamps. If at all possible, avoid overhead lighting, especially fluorescent lighting. The bright light of the sun is wonderful, but indoor brilliance is a shock to the sensitivities of the spirit. If possible, use candles. Not only do candles symbolize God's light, but they also help one to focus. A word of caution:

Do not attempt to light a room solely with candles if you expect people to read or write anything. At least one person (more than likely) will grumble and dampen the mood for the rest of the group.

Accessories

It is most helpful to have objects that will help the participants to attentively focus on the occasion. Try to remove any distracting elements or place such objects off to the side. In the empty space at the front of the semicircle (or in the center of the circle, the leader being part of the circle), place a small piece of rug or carpet or a low table. On it could be flowers, a large plant, a cross, a candle, a Bible, or perhaps objects that speak of the theme (e.g., earthen vessels, a basin of water). Familiar symbols help people focus more easily.

Decor

When leadership teams are especially energized, they can transform a rigid, defined setting into a welcoming environment. This can be accomplished through the use of colored or printed bedsheets as wall hangings (covering some of the permanent and undesirable wall items), paper tablecloths cut for window curtains, easels draped with a quilt or banner as a backdrop, and

indirect lighting placed on the floor behind decorative bags of colored tissue paper. The possibilities are as extensive as one's imagination and creativity—and of course, time.

2. Public Relations

Emphasize the need for *super publicity*. The importance of good public relations cannot be emphasized enough. So many events fall flat because of poor publicity and/or poor communication. It is not sufficient to announce an event only by repeatedly using the same approach and expect an overwhelming response. Like medicines we've taken over the course of time, we can become immune and unresponsive. So the task at hand is to wake people up! Use all forms of communication that presently exist, that is, church newsletters, Sunday worship bulletins, announcements during worship, and posters. But also send personal invitations, as well as letters, to potential attendees. Most helpful will be an extra-large, well-designed colorful poster that conveys the theme, includes a significant design or logo, and is displayed in a well-traveled area in the church. Repeat the design or logo on all communication for easy identification. People will begin to associate this visual element with your event. At the sign-up table, have handouts such as bookmarks with the theme and design or logo found

on the poster, as well as brochures that include the name of the event, time, date, location, contact person(s), and phone number. Appendix A contains sample brochures and handouts.

3. Bibliography

Ask the leader of the event to provide a bibliography of books, tapes, periodicals, and/or videos. Use these resources to promote the event—referring people to items that might be found in the library. Some of the participants may want to prepare for an upcoming event, and a list of resources would assist them in that preparation. The bibliography may also be the basis for a resource table.

4. Resource Display Table

If an event is at all successful, people will want to remember it. One of the best ways to ensure this is to provide information on books and tapes that can help them continue with the experience on their own. Given enough advance time, a church librarian or other volunteer can pull books from the shelves that will reinforce the participants' experiences of an event. The resource display table may also stimulate a consignment of books for purchase. A table or center of resources should be located at a place where people will gather for the break(s) and will be likely to chat about what they see and like. It becomes another "warm" place.

5. Financial Concerns

At the very beginning of the planning session, someone needs to be aware of the financial commitments and logistics. This includes the site reservations for the event (room and place) and any food connected with it. Prices should indicate the total cost and what each person will be charged. Questions that also need to be answered include the following:

- Will the church underwrite any part of the event?
- If engaging a consultant or outside leader for the event, the initial contact should include an agreement or a contract that states his or her fee. What would be a reasonable fee?
- Will the money come from the church's budget, or will it be added to the "per person" charge for the event? Be very clear to all concerned about what is expected.

6. Food and/or Drink Arrangements

Food and/or drink arrangements should be planned well in advance. These arrangements should be made and carried out by persons *not* involved in the event. It is very distracting for a group to have members popping up and down, going in and out, to take care of this and that. In addition, it is most disconcerting to the leader, who is trying to keep the group focused.

7. Personal Touches

Personal touches are the little extras that help people feel comfortable. For the introverts and strangers, name tags are essential; and for those whose memory cannot pull up a name, it is a relief. Be sure the names are written in *large* letters so they can be read. Make sure access to the building and the room are well marked so that people are not frustrated in locating the event. Reproduce the theme with the design or logo on welcome signs, adding directions or arrows.

8. Evaluation

Feedback is vital in terms of future planning, both for the group and the leader. Evaluation forms are usually appropriate at the end of retreats and series. Due to the nature of some events, it is inappropriate to ask people to fill out evaluation forms or give personal feedback lest it destroy a mood or an experience. At such times, the leader and the church liaison person can confer about what they observed as the participants' experiences. Another alternative is to make the evaluation form available during the final break. The term *evaluation* frequently meets with resistance; the term *feedback* is a friendlier word. See appendix C for sample evaluation forms.

▌ Openers

So often we get a group together and jump right in to the task before people are ready to participate or before we have everybody "on board." While there is a growing demand for events that nurture spiritual growth, there is also a definite cautiousness associated with willingness to participate in spirituality events.

The following collection of common questions about spirituality, and excerpts from stories, may help prepare the participants.

▌ Common Questions

1. What's behind our need to slow down?

These spiritual growth events offer a way for people to do just that. Author and psychiatrist Gerald (Jerry) May, Director for Research and Program Development at the Shalem Institute for Spiritual Formation, describes our bodies' response to these busy routines. May believes that the body becomes used to pumping adrenalin and that we, in turn, become physically addicted to our own adrenalin. When we slow down for some quiet time, we experience withdrawal symptoms from our own adrenalin, becoming what he calls "speed pushers!"[1]

2. Why is taking time for spiritual nurture important?

There is an old story about a man who came to a hermit for spiritual direction. His life was full of stress and turmoil, and he claimed that he could no longer find God. The hermit took him down to the river where he silently dipped a bowl into the river, filled it with water, and quietly led him back to his hut. They sat for a very long time until the sand, silt, and mud had gone from churned up to cloudy to clear. The point was made. We, like the man in the story,

need to learn how to sit patiently and wait quietly for our bodies and minds to settle so we can be present to God.

3. What is spirituality anyway? Aren't we offering it through our church programs and worship?

The answer is part yes and part no. Spirituality is a matter of relationship, of having an opportunity to experience God's presence. Most of what the mainline churches offer is related to the knowledge of God and an understanding of the belief systems, along with programs to support this goal. That is not to say that one can't experience God's presence through a study of theology and the Bible. However, most of the time we leave such experiences *in the head*, and they fail to make their way *to the heart*. Spirituality recognizes our hunger for God and is an intentional response to our awareness of God. It enables us to let that awareness accompany us in our work and in our play. It deals with the body, mind, will, imagination, and feelings that may be used as agents of transformation. Anthony de Mello described it as "waking up" as we discover our deep self in God and God in us.[2] It is not information gathering, though some information may be given. Instead, spirituality helps us to focus, to let go of the whirlwind of mental activity, to center on one thing. It helps us to keep out the clutter that fills up our lives. It could be called "relaxing into God" or "wasting time with God." We need to give ourselves permission to do that.

Spirituality events provide us with a time, a place, and a conducive environment with few distractions. All we need, then, is the intent to be open and to listen in silence.

4. What is contemplative prayer?

Contemplative prayer is a way to help us move from an orientation toward *doing* to one of *being*. We know that we cannot work our way into God's favor, so "doing" alone will not ultimately satisfy us. It is learning to rest in who we are and to simply *be*. It is being attentive, yet relaxed; relaxed, yet not asleep. It is a practice that teaches us to be patient with ourselves, that helps us to let go of distractions and interrupting thoughts, and gently returns us to our meditation. It is a means of learning to appreciate silence and of letting go of the need to intellectualize and analyze everything. It teaches patience with what the moment has to offer rather than trying to *make* something happen.

5. What can I expect to happen at these events?

Nothing. There should be no expectations. It will be enough that one is willing to be open to God's presence. Participants are encouraged not to seek any "special feelings" or "results." In fact, the emphasis is on *not* expecting "sound and light shows," since they are frequently misinterpreted. Participants are asked simply to be open and receptive to whatever happens during their time together, realizing that there will be times when nothing seems to be going on, times when a few insights may surface, and times when a session may trigger resistance that needs attention. Be sure that no comparison is made between the experiences of the participants. Each shares only what he or she wants to share. Permission is given to be one's self at all times.

Distractions in the room, outdoors, or inside one's body and mind will frequently demand attention. Learning to let them go and not focus on them is part of the learning process, which is never completely "learned." Jerry May believes that the mind is like an errant child, wandering all around. It needs to be gently called or led back, time after time. Then one can resume with attentiveness to the Word.

6. How do I interpret what happens?

Basically, the answer to this question is in the form of another: Does it draw me closer to God or not? Or look at these words from Jeremiah:

> These are the words of the Lord: Stop at the crossroads; look for the ancient paths; ask, "Where is the way that leads to what is good?" Then take that way, and you will find rest for yourselves. (Jer. 6:16, NEB)

7. Isn't spirituality "too Eastern" in approach?

The roots of Christianity are in the East, where many practices from the early church and from the desert fathers and mothers of the fourth century were once abandoned. Now they are being reclaimed. Even, Jesus himself went apart a while. His quiet time alone most certainly fortified him with the resources he needed to do his ministry. We hardly know what silence is. We need to learn from it.

▌ Excerpts

*Maurice Maeterlinck tells an old parable. It centers on the keeper of a lighthouse on a dangerous coast. Winter was closing in, and the supply boat had not yet arrived with reserves of oil. The few inhabitants of the little village were facing discomfort and possible death in the cold, bleak area, for their individual oil supplies were running out. Because they were his neighbors and because he was a compassionate man, the keeper gave away, little by little, the reserves of oil at the lighthouse. Then one night the bright beacon light went out, and there was no oil to feed the flickering flame. The very supply ship bringing the needed reserves of oil was driven onto the rocky coast and destroyed.

It is only a story, Maeterlinck said, but it suggests this truth about life. We are never to give away the oil of our lamp, be it ever so little. Our gift is the flame. It is blessed to give, but it is also blessed to keep, to reverence our own life. If we do not rest, we soon will not be able to communicate. To give to others, we must keep something for ourselves. Before going out to serve others in the name of God, we let God in to serve and recreate us. "Come away by yourselves to a lonely place, and rest a while."

*Since most of what we learn and hear urges us to hustle, chase, and cram, it takes courage to stop for leisure—and especially to stop for prayer. But what's more wasteful—to push hard until we drop, dead tired, or to be quiet and perhaps touch the depth of life? Isaiah seems to speak to us as we rush around:

> For thus says the Lord God, the Holy One of Israel,
> "In returning and rest you shall be saved;
> in quietness and in trust shall be your strength."
> And you would not, but you said,
> "No! We will speed upon our horses"
> (or cars or planes—or we will just run the rat race).
> (Isa. 30:15–16, RSV)

. . . . The world really doesn't need more busy people, maybe not even more intelligent people. It needs "deep people," people who know that they need solitude if they are going to find out who they are;

> silence, if their words are to mean anything;
> reflection, if their actions are to have any significance;
> contemplation, if they are to see the world as it really is;
> prayer, if they are going to be conscious of God, if they are to
> "know God and enjoy God forever."

The world needs people who want their lives not only to be filled, but to be full and fulfilled.

*Several years ago I began to occasionally attend spiritual retreats at an ecumenical retreat center. These retreats incorporated times of silence as central parts of the retreat experience.

For the first couple of years, I went armed with projects to do during those blocks of silence—letters or papers to write, books to read. That ensured that if there was nothing going on during those times, at least I would have something to do.

I learned from watching others that the silent times were not usually spent on one's knees in fervent prayer. I could take a walk outside and listen to what God was saying to me through the birds and the sky. I could sit by the fireplace and feel the warmth of the fire. In the early hours of a retreat, the silence usually brought a nap.

In the beginning, there was an enormous amount of chatter that had to drain out of my mind before there was any space for quiet. Once there began to be spaces, the silence brought a cleansing. . . .

I greet the silence now with a mixture of fear and excitement, awe and familiarity. Underneath the feelings is a hunger that only the silence can fill, a desire to be held in the quiet arms of God and whispered to in the wind.

*From "Healing," by Emily Wilson, p. 14; reprinted from the Nov/Dec '90 *alive now!* copyright © 1990 by The Upper Room. Used by permission.

*A Trappist friend of mine used to say,
    "It's not enough to apply the brakes on your car;
       you must also cut the motor that's racing inside."
The engine of our solicitudes is still whirring at top speed.
    It has to slacken,
        decelerate
        and turn at an easier pace.
We have to move in time with another rhythm,
       gear our will to another will,
       learn to connect with the slow-paced,
         quiet,
         powerful
         and steady motor of God's will.

As long as we're in turmoil,
       taken up with our problems and our interests,
we're safely sheltered from God
    and out of His reach.
We need several days of recollection
    before we can begin to live in Him
       and on Him.
We have to stay there in a kind of stupor
      and let our motor idle
        till we've adjusted to a new tempo
         we've never experienced before.

If we're too intent on our questionings,
    we can't hear God's answers,
      which are surprising,
        disconcerting,
      and never come to us the way we expect.
To meet God, we have to get away from ourselves.
    Retreatants always stuff their suitcase with a pile of things:
       letters to be answered,
       a book,
       three or four chocolate bars,
       a newspaper
       and a train schedule
        in case the whole business becomes intolerable.
We all feel the need of a few projects
    to shield us from God.
We imagine [God] can't nourish us. . . .

*From Louis Evely, *That Man Is You*, pp. 18–19. Translated by Edmond Bonin. Copyright 1964 by The Missionary Society of St. Paul the Apostle in the State of New York (New York: Paulist Press, 1964). Used by permission.

The Talkative Lover*

A lover pressed his suit unsuccessfully for many months, suffering the atrocious pains of rejections. Finally his sweetheart yielded. "Come to such and such a place, at such and such an hour," she said to him.

At that time and place the lover finally found himself seated beside his beloved. He then reached into his pocket and pulled out a sheaf of love letters that he had written to her over the past months. They were passionate letters, expressing the pain he felt and his burning desire to experience the delights of love and union. He began to read them to his beloved. The hours passed by but still he read on and on.

Finally the woman said, "What kind of a fool are you? These letters are all about me and your longing for me. Well, here I am sitting with you at last. And you are lost in your stupid letters."

"Here I am with you," says God, "and you keep reflecting about me in your head, talking about me with your tongue and searching for me in your books. When will you shut up and see?"

The Great Silence*

"Would you teach me silence?" I asked.

"Ah!"

He seemed to be pleased. "Is it the Great Silence that you want?"

"Yes, the Great Silence."

"Well, where do you think it's to be found?" he asked.

"Deep within me, I suppose. If only I could go deep within, I'm sure I'd escape the noise at last. But it's hard. Will you help me?" I knew he would. I could feel his concern, and his spirit was so silent.

"Well, I've been there," he answered. "I spent years going in. I did taste the silence there. But one day Jesus came—maybe it was my imagination—and said to me simply, 'Come, follow me.' I went out, and I've never gone back."

I was stunned. "But the silence . . ."

"I've found the Great Silence, and I've come to see that the noise was inside."

*From *The Song of the Bird*, by Anthony de Mello, p. 101. Copyright © 1982 by Anthony de Mello, S.J. Used by permission of Doubleday, a division of Bantam Doubleday Dell Publishing Group, Inc.

*From Theophane the Monk, *Tales of a Magic Monastery*, p. 55. Copyright © 1981 by Cistercian Abbey of Spencer, Inc. (New York: Crossroad Publishing Co., 1990). Used with permission of The Crossroad Publishing Company.

▮ Foundations

It is helpful to set a foundation by offering different ways to experience the theme or Scripture so that participants might be able to identify at least one "window to God" that they can take home with them for future use. The following is an overview of a few of these "windows" that can be used as a preparation for prayer, the central focus, or in conjunction with something else.

▮ Silence

The most important foundation that should not be overlooked is silence. Silence is actually *the heart of the matter*.

A period of silence will be observed in all the models throughout this handbook. Some will be strictly for individuals; others, for groups. It may take a while for one to appreciate silence within a group or even to be able to become still physically, mentally, and emotionally. It takes approximately ten minutes for the body to become still. In addition, people become uncomfortable if given more than nine seconds of silence. For beginning groups, silence should be introduced in small doses, since our psyches are not geared to such an extended "shock treatment." For groups that meet on a regular basis to practice silence together, holy kinship often develops. These groups find that they can "center" more quickly than a group that has not practiced silence together.

▮ Guided Relaxation

Guided relaxation is also known as body prayer, body work, or stretching. Its goal is to ease the tension that we carry in our bodies so that we can be more open to the focus of the event.

The scriptural basis for this, as well as suggested practices, may be found in the separate section on pages 22–26.

▮ Breath Prayer

A *breath prayer* is essentially one word or a phrase that is divided into two parts when spoken: The first part is said when you inhale; the second, when you exhale. This can also be used with the suggestion for slower breathing, which will in turn slow the body and mind, thus making a person more receptive or present to God in the stillness. More information on breath prayer is given on page 33.

▮ Presentations

Presentations for the type of spiritual growth events described in this resource do not call for a lecturer or "keynote speaker." The role of the presenter is to offer what is necessary and then to leave space for divine action to take place. The various practices or activities will need to be introduced through some brief background information, an explanation of what to do (or not to do), and perhaps an appropriate example or story. While some presentation time is essential, it is important for the presenter not to dominate the session. This special time together belongs to

God and the participants. One needs to be aware of the fact that words can get in the way of the Word.

▮ Centering

Centering is basically one's desire to reach down into the depth of one's being and experience God's presence. Examples of centering are found in chapter 7 (see Model B. Praying with Scripture [Psalm 139], pages 44–46; Model G. The Jesus Prayer, pages 59–61).

▮ Use of Scripture

While the use of Scripture is not a special approach, it is mentioned here to bring attention to the various ways it can be used. In the organized church, we tend to *read* Scripture in worship services or to engage in Bible study.

Alternative approaches for using Scripture can be found in chapter 7:

1. A centering prayer (see Model B. Praying with Scripture, pages 44–46)
2. Imaging the Word (see Model F. Bartimaeus Dialogue, pages 57–58)
3. Journaling (see Model I. The Rich Young Ruler, pages 63–64)
4. Listening to the Word, Taizé (see Model H. "Stay Here and Watch with Me," pages 61–62).

▮ Chant or Other Music

Music has the power to prime the depths of the soul, to become a doorway into sacred silence. It inspires us, gives us insights into other ways to hear God speaking to us, lets us hear fresh words to familiar passages, introduces us to other cultures, and assists us in centering and getting still. Music can be used either for listening or as a participatory practice like chant. While chants are new to most Protestants, they are used by some contemplative prayer groups and are included in some new hymnals and worship services. Music taken from a variety of ages and genres—from Russian sacred choral music to jazz, from medieval to contemporary music, from panpipes to movie sound tracks—can allow us to be carried into silence and openness to God.

Appropriate music from compact discs and cassette tapes can be used to assist centering. Examples of this music can be found in chapter 7 (see Model L. Sound and Silence, pages 74–79). For a listing of music, see chapter 10 (pages 163–168).

▮ Imaging

Imaging often takes the form of guiding the participants into a scene where they can identify with either the setting (often biblical), or an individual, or a feeling. It may tap into the depths of one's being and unlock doors that need opening. It may provide fresh insights into old situations. It may do nothing except help one to relax. Another approach to imaging is with specific objects whereby the participants see or handle the objects—usually symbols with meaning attached—and picture how they are interacting, that is, a kind of free association. See Model D. Foot Washing (pages 49–53), Model J. A Meditation on Water (pages 65–69) and Model K. A Meditation on Hands (pages 70–73), for examples.

▮ Journaling

Although this can take many forms, from a sectioned notebook to a simple piece of paper, the technique basically calls for one to record responses. It may be asking for the following:

- a simple paragraph about what was experienced during a period of silence
- a record of feelings encountered after taking a walk
- a response to Scripture

There is no limit. Journaling is a way to unleash thoughts and feelings that might otherwise be elusive. There may be surprises, intuitive discoveries, pain and healing, release, and rejoicing. A journal may be used to write prayers, insights from dreams, and new directions for living. Most people are surprised to discover that they will sometimes write things down that they had not consciously thought about.

Journaling *is* a tool, not necessarily *the* tool. People need to be encouraged in small ways to learn its benefits.

One very definite aid to the beginner's experience is to provide groups with journal booklets. These booklets should have an attractive cover that incorporates the theme of the activity and two or three blank pages inside that are stapled or folded together. The journal booklet should be sized to fit in a Bible, a book, or a purse. If kept, as they usually are, journals can be referred to in later months or years to note one's growth. Journal writing is used in almost every event in this handbook. Journal ideas, as well as sample covers, may be found in appendix B. Additional materials to assist one in understanding or exploring journaling are listed in chapter 10.

A meditation booklet can be used for reflection and response. This booklet can provide selections that call one to prayer, give comments to reflect on, use quotes from books one might want to read, and incorporate material that relates to the theme of the retreat.

▮ Worship

In all events, there will be some form of programmed worship experience, such as morning prayer or opening worship, grace at meals, vespers, or closing worship and communion. Most of these should be planned well in advance, the exception being the closing worship of a retreat. At the closing worship of a retreat, the participants should be given an opportunity to assimilate their various experiences and to find ways to share them in their final time together. Invariably this will prove to be the most meaningful part of a retreat. Additional suggestions on retreats may be found in chapter 8.

▮ Getting Still

In the rush of our busy lives, even attending to business of the church, we usually arrive in a state of hurry, worry, or preoccupation. Prior to your meetings, have the participants find their own quiet place or private space, so that they may be attentive to God's Spirit—the source of inspiration and guidance.

Somewhere I read that unlike the Quakers, who are silent until they feel moved to speak, we speak with abandon until told to be quiet! Perhaps we can practice some silence and "listening prayer" prior to our gatherings, so that during the meeting time we might experience the Quaker "leading" that inspires us to speak from that holy source.

Participants should remain quiet for at least fifteen minutes, since it takes the body about ten minutes to be fully at rest. Setting aside twenty minutes for silence, followed by five minutes of intercessory prayer, is even more desirable (see "A Preparation for Listening Prayer" on page 21).

A Preparation for Listening Prayer

With our bodies and minds active all day, we can hardly expect our inner selves to be naturally still when we sit down for prayer. Thoughts dash about in our heads as we remember something we forgot to do, an appointment we want to make, or a conversation we had. Since we experience so little of silence, silent moments tend to be only another time we can continue to use our busy minds.

To allow ourselves to become still and experience the quiet mind that is open to God, let us take a few moments to consciously prepare ourselves to listen to what God is saying to us.

Here are a few suggestions that may be helpful. None of these is guaranteed to prevent distracting thoughts or drifting minds, but each offers a focus to help in "centering." As external thoughts intrude, just let them go and gently return to your place of quiet.

1 Shut your eyes and be conscious of your breathing. Now, gradually slow your breathing as you feel yourself to be a part of all creation, realizing that into *you* God blew the breath of life.

2 As you inhale, picture yourself being filled with God's love, forgiveness, and mercy. As you exhale, picture all the problems or concerns in your life drifting away.

3 Repeat to yourself Psalm 62:1: "For God alone my soul waits in silence."

4 See the candle flame as an extension of your heart, burning to have deeper communion with the Holy One and to be filled with this Light that gives life.

5 Offer to God all the thoughts, concerns, and barriers that keep you from wanting to listen. Ask for whatever forgiveness you think you need at this time; then listen—and accept the grace and mercy of God that brings wholeness and peace.

"Be still, and know that I am God!"
(Ps. 46:10)

❚ Guided Relaxation

❚ An Introduction to Body Prayer

. . . do you not know that your body is a temple of the Holy Spirit within you, which you have from God, and that you are not your own? For you were bought with a price; therefore glorify God in your body.

(1 Cor. 6:19–20)

We know that our bodies are part of our whole being. Popular books by Bernie Siegel, Norman Cousins, Joan Borysenko, and Caroline Myss affirm this position. Our bodies reflect much of what is going on inside us, and very often we are far from relaxed.

We want to allow our bodies (and whole selves) to relax in God's loving presence. Are our bodies stiff and tense? If so, our hearts and minds may then be in knots! Though we can have a willingness for God's presence in the midst of knots, we might find it easier without them. We frequently pray *for* our bodies, yet rarely do we pray *with* them, using them in our prayer. Our goal, then, is to release tension, to open ourselves more fully to God, and to become more conscious and attentive. The following examples are not unique. They are basic movements that can be found anywhere. The only difference is that we do not do them as an

"exercise." Instead, we move with an awareness and a slowed-down pace that assists us in being present to the Creator. With that in mind, each movement can be a prayer, a response to the Holy Spirit within.

1. Slowing the breath

Do this five times. This is one of the best introductory exercises. People are able to sit and concentrate on their breathing without much resistance. Once they have slowed down a bit, they generally will be more receptive to other forms of relaxation. Remind them that life is in the breath.

What follows are six steps to the "complete breath":

- Exhale, pulling in your abdomen.
- Inhale, distending your abdomen (taking in as much air as possible).
- Continue inhaling, now filling and expanding your chest area.
- Continue to inhale, raising your shoulders upward.
- Hold, retaining the posture, for the count of five.
- Then exhale again, relaxing your shoulders and chest while contracting your abdomen.

2. A sitting exercise

- Wiggle your right ankle.
- Gradually raise your right leg until you feel your spine stretching.
- Lower your right leg slowly and repeat.
- Do the same with your left leg.

3. Shoulder stretch
(can be done sitting or standing)

- Lift your right shoulder up, around toward your back, then down, up in the front, and back to its original position; this will be a circular motion. Repeat three times.
- Do the same with your left shoulder, then do both shoulders together.

4. Notice any tight places

Take a moment to notice any tight places in your body. Pay attention to them. Massage or move them. Bend, if necessary, to loosen them up.

5. Loosen neck area

- With hands on your hips, slowly move your head toward your right shoulder three times.
- Then move your head toward your left shoulder three times.

6. Neck roll or rotation

Let your head move toward your right shoulder, slightly toward your back, toward your left shoulder, and then to the front. Be very careful when moving your head to the back; it is a sensitive area. Reverse direction.

7. Waist bend (or side bend)

With hands on your hips, bend from the waist first to the right, then back slightly, then to the left, and finally to the front. This is a circular motion. Reverse the direction.

8. Slowing the breath while standing

- Stand and do the same complete breath exercise as described in exercise 1, above.
- Place your feet together, making sure your arms and trunk are limp.
- As you inhale, expand your abdomen and raise your arms slowly, with palms upward, and touch your hands over your head.
- Reach up slightly on toes and hold to a count of five.
- Exhale slowly with palms face down and resume former posture.

9. The Rag Doll

- Take three deep breaths.
- Stand straight with your feet slightly apart (in line with your shoulders).
- Let your arms float upward until they're over your head.
- Stretch, reach for God, your desire.
- Tilt your head back until you can feel a slight bit of tension in your lower back.
- Gradually bend your arms and torso forward and downward, as far as it is comfortable (like a rag doll).
- Gradually, vertebra by vertebra, begin to straighten your body to a standing position.
- Have participants repeat the exercise, listening again to the directions. Then ask them to repeat the exercise three times on their own.

10. Back stretch

- Stand with your hands on your upper thighs, then reach upward with your arms and bend slightly backward.
- Gradually bend your arms and torso forward and downward. Feel your spine stretching. Notice your arms.
- With your hands on your knees, bend your elbows; move your hands toward your calves, your ankles, and then your feet.
- Keeping your forehead down and your knees straight, continue stretching. Do not strain; only do what you can, comfortably.
- Moving very slowly, raise yourself to an upright position and repeat the exercise.

11. Meditation Exercises

(Used with Psalm 139)

- Relax, breathe slowly; recollect yourself.
- Hug yourself.
- Then very slowly, kneel and lean back on your feet, resting there.
- Bow your head, then lean it toward the right, the back, the left, the front, and repeat.
- Lie down on the floor; bring your arms and legs upward and inward into a fetal position.
- Roll from side to side very slowly.
- Stretch out on your back; be open; feel exposed; notice your body sensations.

(Used with "A Meditation on Hands")

- Stand straight, but relaxed with your arms outstretched, but elbows slightly bent.
- Turn your palms upward in a gesture of offering and receiving.
- Bend slightly back with your chin near your chest. Breathe deeply and notice your hands.
- Then come back to your original position.

(Used with "A Meditation on Hands")

- Clench fists tightly. Grasp. Clutch. Hold.
- Relax hands; feel the release of tension, the letting go.
- Repeat.

The two body prayers on pages 25–26 are suitable for general openings and closings, as well as for children, since they are simple to learn and repeat.

Group Body Prayer*

1 Hold hands in prayerful gesture; be in an attitude of prayer.

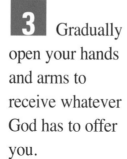

2 Slowly raise praying hands up above your head.

Let your eyes follow your hands.

Let this be a symbol of your desire for God, your reaching out to be present to God.

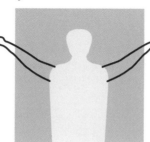

3 Gradually open your hands and arms to receive whatever God has to offer you.

4 Very slowly bring your arms down to your heart, crossing one over the other.

Bring the gifts from God to your heart.

Cherish them, hold them there. Express gratitude.

5 Now open your arms; stretch them out toward those who are next to you.

Give your gift away. Offer it to the world.

Share God's love to you with others.

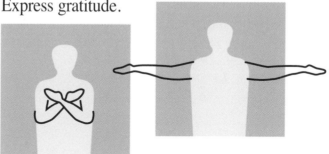

*With thanks to Gerald May, Director for Research and Program Development, Shalem Institute for Spiritual Formation, Bethesda, Maryland.

Celebration*

I am a delight to God my Creator.   (Throw arms out like a child filled with joy.)

I am embraced by Christ Jesus the Son.   (Embrace self, crossing arms over chest.)

I am a masterpiece-in-the-making   (Hold hands together, palms up, as though
                 holding a precious gift.)

 of God's Creative Holy Spirit.   (Hands reach straight up, eyes following.)

*With thanks to Pastor Alan Mugler of Gaithersburg Presbyterian Church, Gaithersburg, Maryland. Please note that this body prayer has been adapted.

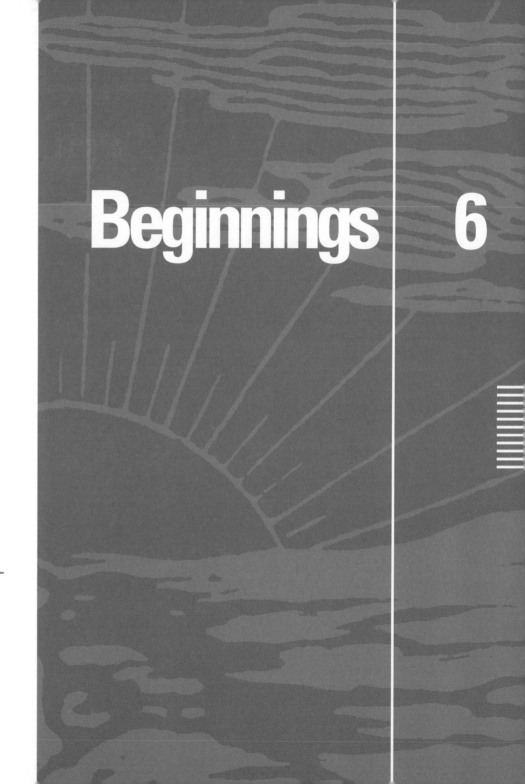

Beginnings 6

▎ Community Building— A Reflective Model (30 minutes)

This reflective model can be used to assist the participants in being open to God's word and presence and to experience being one in the Spirit.

▎ Opening

Sing "They'll Know We Are Christians by Our Love," and then introduce the theme for the meeting (for example, "A New Commandment").

▎ Small Group

Have each participant count off by the numbers one, two, and three, so three people will be in each group. Give each group one of the Scripture passages on page 29, along with a copy of the directions "Meditation on Scripture" (page 30). Tell everyone to follow the directions and to share within their own group. After a designated time (perhaps ten minutes), ask the groups to come back to form the larger group.

▎ Large Group

Once the participants are reassembled in the larger group, ask for a volunteer to read the assigned passage and share one key insight that came from his or her small group.

▎ Prayer

In advance, ask someone to lead a prayer that allows the participants to express their intercessions or concerns or thanksgivings.

▎ Closing

Sing "This Is My Commandment" (Bible school song) or one of your own choosing.

Scripture Passages

Cut apart and give one passage to each small group.
The noted translation is preferred.

This is how all will know you for my disciples, if you have love for one another. (John 13:35, NAB)	If I speak in human and angelic tongues, but do not have love, I am a resounding gong, a clashing cymbal. (1 Cor. 13:1, NAB)
This is my commandment: love one another as I love you. (John 15:12, NAB)	Love is patient; love is kind; love is not envious or boastful or arrogant. (1 Cor.13:4, NRSV)
If someone says he loves God, yet hates his brother, he is a liar. For he cannot love God, whom he has not seen, if he does not love his brother, whom he has seen. (1 John 4:20, TEV)	Love is not rude. It does not insist on it own way; it is not irritable or resentful. (1 Cor. 13:5, NRSV)
We love because God first loved us. (1 John 4:19, NRSV)	Owe nothing to anyone except to love one another; for the one who loves another has fulfilled the law. (Romans 13:8, NAB)
My children, our love should not be just words and talk; it must be true love, which shows itself in action. (1 John 3:18, TEV)	God is not unfair. He will not forget the work you did, or the love you showed . . . in the help you gave and are still giving to your fellow Christians. (Heb. 6:10, TEV)

Meditation on Scripture

1 Listen carefully while this passage is read to you at least three times.

2 Close your eyes and let it sink into your subconscious.

If you start to shift gears, gently bring yourself back to the passage by remembering the word *love* in the passage.

3 Be still and open to what God might be saying to you in these words.

Don't force yourself to "think" about it. Just relax (for five minutes) and let it become part of your breathing.

4 Open your eyes. Jot down any insights you felt might have been conveyed to you.

Silence—The Other Half of Prayer
(90 minutes)

Music is playing as people arrive, get seated and settle down. (One excellent suggestion for music is Daniel Kobialka's extended version of Bach's "Jesu, Joy of Man's Desiring.")[1] Position chairs in a circle or semicircle with a candle in the center.

Opening Introductions
(5 minutes)

Initial Remarks
(approximately 3 minutes)

The initial remarks are printed here as an example. These remarks should be tailored to fit the leader's experience.

I am pleased to be able to join you in thinking about a subject that has followed me throughout my life. Just recently I was led to reflect on moments that influenced my faith journey and recalled my teenage years at youth conferences. We had what was called *Morning Watch*. We were supposed to take our printed devotional material for the day to some spot where we could be alone and where we could use it for reflection and prayer. At that age, socializing was decidedly more important, and I have memories of the days when I yielded to the temptation to skip it and visit with friends. But I always knew that I was cheating myself, because I valued that silence way back then.

The temptation is the same today—only in a different form. I still resist taking the time for quiet and reflection when so many other things beckon. And, after all, the people in my life can be verbally demanding. God can't be seen or heard, so I can dismiss God more easily. Maybe not. I know I am still cheating myself if I do.

Maybe you bring similar issues with you. We all seem to struggle with prayer in one way or another. I remember hearing the Sunday school superintendent pray during opening exercises when I was growing up. He had a very strong, impressive voice and prayed with all the Thee's and Thou's in place, as well as what I considered all the "right" phrases for addressing the Deity. I knew I could never pray like that. And I don't. But I have learned to expand my views on prayer. I hope to share some of them with you today.

▋ Explanations
(3 minutes)

Hand out journal booklets and pencils if needed. Read aloud the following or state it in your own words.

This journal is to record your spiritual journey. No one will see what is written here except you who are writing. Nor will you be expected to share anything unless you choose to do so.

One thing I ask of you is to give yourself permission to spend some time with God during the next hour or so.

The value of being in a circle is a feeling of unity, community, connected feeling, energy, focus.

The importance of the candle is that it represents God in our midst, the Light of the world and the Light within us— Christ in you. You can do the same thing at home, choosing a symbol that calls your attention to a special place where you expect to be with God. You can associate this place and time with your desire for God.

▋ Presentation
(15 minutes)

Read aloud the following or state it in your own words.

Whenever we take the time to pay attention to our spiritual life, we are usually filled with feelings of failure. We end up seeing our shortcomings. We see our desire without the follow-through. Then we berate ourselves for not having better prayer habits or devotional time. But underneath, the desire is still there. That desire is not our own. It is placed there by God. It reflects God's desire for us. Facing our shortcomings is a way of refocusing, because in doing so we confess our desire to be in closer relationship with God.

We will be spending time together with that desire for God and looking at ways we can nurture, tend, recognize, and sustain that desire. You will probably not be receptive or comfortable with everything that is offered, but I hope you will find one or two "windows" opening up that you will want to remember, take home, and repeat.

When we think of our prayer life, we often remember past instruction. For many of us, we grew up learning formulas for prayer like ACTS (adoration, confession, thanksgiving, and supplication). And we've taught our own children to *say* prayers, to *say* grace.

Somewhere, though, we were also taught that prayer is a two-way street, a conversation with God, or keeping company with God. But we keep the banter going, "Thank you . . . Bless . . . Guide . . . Help . . . May I . . . Please would you . . . Dear Lord . . ." and so on.

Wouldn't you hate being on God's end of our prayers? If we do all the talking, how can it be prayer?

Prayer is not words. Prayer is a *relationship*. If we keep God from participating in this relationship, how can we know *what is of God and what is not of God*? How can we feel the nudges or receive an insight or become inspired? We are like the Greek Diadochus, who spoke of the steambath.

When the door of the steambath is continually left open, the heat inside rapidly escapes through it; likewise the soul, in its desire to say many things, dissipates its remembrance of God through the door of speech, even though everything it says may be good. Thereafter the intellect, though lacking appropriate ideas, pours out a welter of confused thoughts to anyone it meets, as it no longer has the Holy Spirit to keep its understanding free from fantasy.[2]

Author Henri Nouwen continues to say that our lifestyle of sharing has "become one of the greatest virtues," including everything we can possibly verbalize.[3] We are forever leaving the door to the steambath open—that is, our mouths.

And so it is. Our prayer life is like our everyday life. We are not good listeners. In a conversation or discussion, we wait for an opening so we can jump in with our own thoughts and ideas. In prayer, unlike the Quakers who are silent until they feel moved to speak, we speak with abandon until we are told to be still. When we try to be still and listen, all we hear are our laundry lists of things to do, giving us an update or an assessment. Or we find ourselves reviewing our concerns for self and others, worrying about this and that. We are still listening to *ourselves*.

It takes ten to twelve minutes before the body and mind slow down from their busyness so that we can be fully attentive to God. (*Note:* Consider reading or telling the story of the hermit, page 13, or The Talkative Lover, page 17.)

Now we are going to experience two forms of breath prayer that will help us slow down and be attentive. The first will be through the spirit in us, our breath, along with Scripture. The second will be through praying the psalms.

▍ Breath Prayer
(35 minutes)

Read aloud the following. The directions will take approximately five to eight minutes.

To become still, it is important to pay attention to our posture and our body language. We want to convey our openness through our body. Sitting with the spine straight, one's feet flat on the floor, an attitude of alertness—all these are helpful.

I will lead you into this time together; then we will have five to ten minutes of silence. I will ring a bell to indicate we are finished. (*Note:* Read the following *very* slowly.)

Close your eyes. . . .
Pay attention to your breath. . . .
Breath is spirit, life. . . .
God blew into us the breath of
    life. . . .
Note your holy breath. . . .
Watch it. . . .
Follow it . . . .
In and out. . . .

Slowing down to listen is difficult because we need to slow the body, which depends on the breath. Mostly we breathe short, shallow breaths. They don't go anywhere. We end up hyperventilating a lot of the time. Take time to breathe real deeply and slowly—all the way down to the abdomen. Fill it with God's breath of life, the supreme gift.

Now inhale all that is of God, and exhale all that seems not to be of God.

Keep your eyes closed. Keep breathing. While you are slowing your breath, I will read the familiar verse from Psalm 46:10: "Be still and know that I am God." This will be our breath prayer.

As you inhale, hear the words "*Be still*." As you exhale, hear the words "*and know*."

Inhale, exhale. Be still/and know. Keep repeating the phrase to yourself in the silence. If your mind wanders, do not be discouraged. Just bring it back gently as you would a wandering child, and take its hand and try again.

"Be still . . .
and know. . . . "

▌ Silence
(5 or 10 minutes)

(*Note:* The more time you have available to do this activity, the better.)

Ring a bell. Ask the participants the following questions, having them write their reflections in their journals. Allow about five minutes for the participants to write down their responses.

1. How did this simple breath prayer help you to be present to God?
2. If you experienced difficulty or resistance, what was that like?

Ask the participants to share any part of this experience with the person next to them. Allow about ten minutes for people to share. Then ask each participant to give a Scripture verse that could be a breath prayer. Allow about five minutes for people to exchange Scripture verses.

▌ Short Group Time
(5 minutes)

List on newsprint the Scripture verses that people received from their partner. Then hand out the sheet "Breath Prayer Suggestions" (page 36) for them to take home.

▌ Writing Your Own Psalm
(15 minutes)

Read aloud the following or state in your own words.

At this time I would like you to write in your journal (or draw on paper if you are a right-brained person who prefers the visual to the verbal) what is going on in your life right now. This will *not* be shared. Begin by saying, "Dear God." Write your feelings, whether you like them or not. Be honest. Who are we kidding by coming to God with sweet talk when our heart is in a rage or a depression? We think we're not being good Christians when we rant at God, but consider how our pent-up bodies and dishonest souls wreak havoc on others. Tell God all about your anger, your joys, your frustrations, your unanswered questions, your grief. Ask God anything you like.

(*Allow about ten minutes for people to write or draw.*)

▌ Praying the Psalms
(15 minutes)

Distribute copies of Psalms 13 and 40 (see page 37). Tell the group that these psalms are taken from an inclusive language version based on the Grail translation from the Hebrew. Ask the participants to take time to read these two psalms. Say to them the following:

Let the words of the psalms become your words. Let your eyes find a word or phrase that best expresses your feelings right now. Let the words sink in. Read it several times. Close your eyes and rest with those words, knowing that God is present with you, ready to touch you in the deep places with comfort, healing, acceptance, and unconditional love. Be open to whatever comes in the silence.

(*In approximately ten minutes, ring bell.*)

▌ Reflective Writing
(5–10 minutes)

Ask the participants to write in their journals what these two experiences (writing their own psalms and praying the psalms) were like for them. Tell them that their reflections will be for their own private record, not for sharing. Then ask these questions:

1. Where was God?
2. Were you aware of a desire for God or of any resistance to meeting God in this way?

▌ Concluding Remarks and Circle
(10 minutes)

Read aloud the following or state in your own words.

We can write our own feelings and psalms at any time; and we can use the psalms from the Bible to comfort, encourage, give thanks, and offer praise. They speak to "wherever we are." My friend Jennifer Santley, with whom I shared leadership of a Lenten series, spoke these words when referring to the psalms:

Jesus used the psalms to express his feelings to God, even from the cross (Psalm 22). The psalmist knew that any kind of suffering is the stuff of which prayers are made. Nothing in human experience is alien to God; nothing lies outside God. And anything raised in honesty to God in prayer is somehow transformed. We might find ways of praying the psalms that match our experience. At times the psalms of praise and thanksgiving may seem right; at others, a quiet expression of trust in God seems appropriate; or we may be in need of some good hard lamenting. When all is said and done and we have poured out our hearts to God, in joy and in sorrow, we realize that it isn't just a resignation to circumstances but an expression of confidence in God's dependable presence. Our hope is rooted in God, not in the circumstances.

▌ Closing
(10 minutes)

Sing "Spirit of the Living God."

Use one of the body prayers with motion (pages 25 and 26). Then have a prayer circle: intercessory prayer. Begin with silence for ourselves, then say aloud the names and places of others where there is need.

Breath Prayer Suggestions

Choose/life (Deut. 30:19)

The Lord/goes before [me] (Deut. 31:8)

Beside still water/the Lord leads me (Psalm 23)

Be still before the Lord/wait patiently (Ps. 37:7)

Be still/and know (Ps. 46:10)

For God alone/my soul waits in silence (Ps. 62:1)

In quietness and in trust/shall be [my] strength (Isa. 30:15)

I have called you by name/you are mine (Isa. 43:1)

Lord Jesus Christ/have mercy on me

      or Lord/have mercy (The Jesus Prayer)

Breathe on me/breath of God (hymn)

Fill me/with life anew (hymn)

Jesus loves me!/this I know (hymn)

Psalm 13: A Prayer of One in Anxiety*

How long, O Lord, will you forget me?

How long will you hide your face?

How long must I bear grief in my soul,

this sorrow in my heart day and night?

How long shall my enemy prevail?

Look at me, answer me, Lord my God!

Give light to my eyes lest I fall asleep in death,

lest my enemy say: "I have prevailed";

lest my foes rejoice to see my fall.

As for me, I trust in your merciful love.

Let my heart rejoice in your saving help.

Let me sing to the Lord for his goodness to me,

singing psalms to the name of the Lord, the Most High.

*From *The Psalms: An Inclusive Language Version Based on the Grail Translation from the Hebrew*, p. 13. Copyright © 1963, 1986 Ladies of the Grail (England). Used by permission of G.I.A. Publications, Inc., Chicago, Illinois, exclusive agent. All rights reserved.

Psalm 40: A Song of Praise*

I waited, I waited for the Lord

and he stooped down to me;

he heard my cry.

He drew me from the deadly pit,

from the miry clay.

He set my feet upon a rock

and made my footsteps firm.

He puts a new song into my mouth,

praise of our God.

Many shall see and fear

and shall trust in the Lord. . . .

*From *The Psalms: An Inclusive Language Version Based on the Grail Translation from the Hebrew*, pp. 54–55. Copyright © 1963, 1986 Ladies of the Grail (England). Used by permission of G.I.A. Publications, Inc., Chicago, Illinois, exclusive agent. All rights reserved.

Prayer Experience Models

7

▎ Prayer Experience Models
(1–2 hours each)

The thirteen prayer experience models presented in this chapter are based on the models used by the Shalem Institute for Spiritual Formation and also includes information drawn from my own experience.[1]

1. Enter in Silence and Prayer

Sit in a circle with a candle in the center of the room. The value of the circle is to emphasize unity and to promote community. The candle represents God in our midst, the Light of the world, and the Light within. Strike a small bell to begin.

2. Guided Relaxation/ Body Prayer
(5–10 minutes)

3. Brief Presentation
(10–15 minutes)

4. Silence
(15–20 minutes)

A beginning group may need to start with ten minutes of silence. This is about the time when the body begins to get still. Gradually expand the time in later sessions to fifteen minutes, so that the group can experience the fullness of silence. Helpful hints for this period of time include sitting erect and not slouching; keeping feet flat on the floor; being aware of the breath; and being open to the experience.

5. Rest and Journaling
(5–10 minutes)

In a way, the journal is the "text" for the time together. It does not replace Scripture, but symbolizes an intent of drawing out firsthand experience with God, surrounded by Scripture. See page 185 for more ideas.

6. Reflection Questions
(5–10 minutes)

It will be necessary to keep questions concise and to repeat them slowly for people to write down.

7. Small Group Sharing
(10–15 minutes)

Depending on the setting and the amount of time available, small group sharing could mean breaking into designated groups of three to five, self-grouping, or simply turning to the adjacent person in the circle. Permission should always be given not to share in the small group if that is one's preference. The sharing is intended to center around the reflection questions and is not a "free-for-all" kind of sharing that includes personal problems and concerns. It is to be focused on one's presence for God and on that relationship—no other. It is important to allow each person to have some time, not permitting any one person to dominate the group time. Each person's contribution is as valuable as another's; no one "experience" or "insight" should be allowed to captivate the group to the extent that it minimizes the value of others' time with God. In the beginning, the leader should circulate slowly and quietly among the small groups to ensure that this guideline is being followed.

8. Plenary
(5–15 minutes)

Individuals may wish to share an insight they learned from the small group time. Sometimes a new question is raised in the larger gathering or additional contributions are offered for the total group.

9. Closing Prayer Circle
(5–10 minutes)

The group circle can hold hands or have a group hug, whichever feels more comfortable. If this seems too intimate in the beginning, then the group should feel free to simply stand in place. The leader opens the prayer, then leads the group into voluntary intercessory prayer—perhaps naming subjects (causes, concerns, places, those that need healing or wholeness, etc.) that might be prayed for. At the end, the leader might offer a sentence prayer that each person in turn will pass to the person on his or her left, addressing each by name (for example, passing the peace: "Amy, may the peace of Christ go with you this week"). This necessitates learning the name of the person to the left. The leader could end the prayer with a blessing or lead the group in one of the group body prayers with motions (pages 25 and 26).

10. Homework

If desired, an assignment may be given to help participants reinforce or "stay with" whatever was presented at that session.

▌ Adaptations

- Sometimes a shorter session is desired to open or close a meeting or gathering. These sessions can be adapted for such occasions by using only part of the theme, less silence, sharing with the person next to you, and then having a closing prayer/ benediction/passing of the peace.
- These models can serve as components of a retreat. They can be incorporated into a theme or used to introduce a different way of viewing prayer.
- Different passages of Scripture can be used with the same model.
- A series can be built around a group of these sessions.
- The prayer experience models that follow are "starters" only. Their possibilities are endless. Simply remember to honor one critical ingredient: the silence. That is basically where the strength of the session lies.
- The prayer experience models may be used in any order. It is suggested, however, that one begin with the first two in order to become acquainted with the breath prayer and the use of Scripture in a contemplative setting.[2]

Model
A

▌ Breath Prayer from Scripture (Psalm 62:1)

▌ Guided Relaxation/ Body Prayer (5–10 minutes)

See pages 22–26 for suggestions.

▌ Brief Presentation (10–15 minutes)

Additional material can be found in "Silence—The Other Half of Prayer" (pages 31–35).

Read aloud the following or state in your own words.

1. Our breath is a sign of life, of creation, of God's Spirit (Genesis).
2. Deep, open breathing helps us express our acceptance of life. Tense, short breaths usually accompany anger and frustration.
3. Paying attention to our breath can help us notice our emotions.
4. Watching the breath focuses our attention and calms the mind.

Author Anthony de Mello tells of a Jesuit friend who sought instructions from a Hindu guru in the art of prayer.

The guru said to him, *"Concentrate on your breathing."* My friend proceeded to do just that for about five minutes. Then the guru said, *"The air you breathe is God. You are breathing God in and out. Become aware of that, and stay with that awareness."*

My friend . . . followed these instructions—for hours on end, day after day—and discovered, to his amazement, that prayer can be as simple a matter as breathing in and out. And he discovered in this exercise a depth and satisfaction and spiritual nourishment that he hadn't found in the many, many hours he had devoted to prayer over a period of many years.[3]

Psalm 150:6 says, "Let everything that breathes praise God!" That is what we are going to do. It is what we call the "Breath Prayer."

Directions
(with many long pauses)

Ask participants to get into a comfortable position, but not so comfortable that they prefer to sleep! Their backs should be straight, with their feet flat on the floor. No slouching. Ask them to let their bodies demonstrate that they are open and attentive, ready to listen and receive what comes.

Tell participants that you will lead them into this exercise, which will be followed by fifteen minutes of silence. You will ring a bell to indicate that the time is over and then give further directions. Ask participants to close their eyes, while you say the following:

Pay attention to the breath.
Breath is spirit, life.
In Genesis we remember that God blew
    into us the breath of life.
Note this holy breath.
Watch it, follow it . . . in and out.

Slowing down to listen or feel God's
    presence is difficult because we need
    to slow down the body, too, . . .
    which depends on the breath.
Mostly we breathe short, shallow
    breaths.
They don't go anywhere.
We end up hyperventilating much of the
    time.

Notice how you inhale and exhale.
Follow these.
To help you notice them more, count
    them.
Begin breathing slowly and more deeply.

Notice that the deeper breaths come
    from the lower abdominal area.
Fill it with God's breath of life, the
    supreme gift.

Inhale with the intent of inhaling God's
    spirit, all that God is for you.
Exhale what is not of God or that which
    stands between you and God.

(*Allow another three minutes for this.*)

Keep breathing deeply and slowly.
Now I will give you a verse of
    Scripture to inhale and exhale
    (Psalm 62:1).

"For God alone/my soul waits in
    silence."

Inhale on the first part of the verse;
    exhale on the second part.

(*Repeat the verse twice*)

Now be silent.

▌ Silence
(15–20 minutes)

▌ Rest and Journaling
(5–10 minutes)

Ask the participants to record in their journals any thoughts and images they had during the silence.

▌ Reflection Questions
(5–10 minutes)

Ask the participants to ponder the following questions and respond to them in their journals.

    1. Did this exercise help you in being present with God or at least desirous of God?

    2. Did you experience any resistance? What was that like?

    3. How might this exercise tie in with your daily quiet time and life in general?

▌ Small Group Sharing
(10–15 minutes)

Ask the participants to share their responses in pairs or small groups.

▌ Plenary
(5–15 minutes)

Ask the participants to share an insight they learned from the small group sharing.

▌ Closing Prayer Circle
(5–10 minutes)

Ask the participants to gather in a circle for prayer. Refer to page 41 for suggestions.

Homework

Ask the participants to use one of these phrases of Scripture during the week, inhaling on the first part of the verse and exhaling on the last part.

- Psalm 46:10—Be still/and know (or "and know that I am God!")
- Isaiah 43:1—Do not fear/I have redeemed you.
- Isaiah 43:1—I have called you by name/you are mine.
- Isaiah 30:15—In quietness and in trust/shall be my strength
- Isaiah 43:4—You are precious in my sight/and I love you.
- Isaiah 43:5—Do not fear/I am with you.

Or hand out "Breath Prayer Suggestions" from page 36 and have them select one for the week.

Model

B

Praying with Scripture (Psalm 139)

Read aloud the following or state in your own words.

In focusing on Scripture, we recognize that many stories combine to tell One Story. We are also aware that our own story is part of that whole Story.

Guided Relaxation/ Body Prayer (5–10 minutes)

See page 24 for suggestions relating to this psalm.

Brief Presentation (10–15 minutes)

Read aloud the following or state in your own words.

An Introduction to Praying with Scripture

From the silence comes the Word.

Connectedness to words are found in the Scripture, in the biblical passages both familiar and unfamiliar. The words, the sounds vibrate us into being and call us by name. They lead us to biblical prayer.

We are not trying to master the content, but are allowing ourselves to be mastered by the One who comes through Scripture to minister to us. Praying with Scripture is bringing our heart to God, letting the words become a vehicle for our transformation.

Our goal, then, is to be guided by the living Spirit of God through the words. Even though the words are familiar, we want to approach the words with openness, as though we never heard them before. Our mind is fresh, yearning to hear what we need to hear.

Isaac of Syria said we should read the spaces as well as the words of Scripture. Words are the shaping of the vast spaces of God. Let the words guide us to God; let the words carry us to that Presence.

We don't have to understand what it all means. Isaiah tells us that the words, like the rain, will not return empty.[4]

Background of Psalm 139

Read aloud the following or state in your own words.

It has been said that Psalm 139 is "prayer in a stillness in which the soul and God are alone." A beautiful phrase is found only in this psalm and nowhere else in the Old Testament—"wings of the morning" (wings of the dawn), pointing to the rapidity with which the light of early morning spreads over the sky. This psalm has been used by those facing death as well as those desiring strength in the midst of life's problems. The author is anonymous. Unlike the psalms that relate to the exile, this one is very personal. Much is written about

our search for God, but not much is written about the Almighty's knowledge of and search for us. Sooner or later we give in to the light that draws us and begs us to be known as we are.

Directions

Read aloud the following or state in your own words.

In praying with Scripture, we will use a method called *Lectio Divina* (pronounced: lexio diveena), which means "divine reading." (For more on *Lectio Divina*, see sample in Retreat Theme 1. Simple Gifts, page 104.) It involves four steps: reading, reflection, prayer, and resting. The resting may also be called a "letting go" or experiencing the still presence.

Listen to the passage as it is read the first time, noticing any words or phrases that seem to stand out in a special way for you. On the second reading, listen for a word that might "shimmer" for you and let it become your word or phrase to reflect on. From there let your word or phrase sink into your being, letting it touch you as it will. Pray that God will use this word or phrase to bring you closer or show you what is called for in your life. Finally, allow yourself to rest with impressions, words, and any images or feelings that may have arisen.

Be guided by the living Spirit of God through the words of the psalm. Even though much of the passage may be familiar to you, listen as though you have never heard it before—with a fresh mind, yearning to hear what is needful for you. Let the words carry you into that Holy Presence. Be aware of any phrase or word that stands out and speaks to you. Retain it. Be with it during the silence. May the words of the passage be a prayer through which you and God are present together.

(Read Psalm 139 from three of the following suggested Bible versions.)

The New Revised Standard Version
The Psalms: An Inclusive Language
Version Based on the Grail
Translation from the Hebrew[5]
The Psalms: A New Translation for
Prayer and Worship[6]
The New Jerusalem Bible
Psalms/Now[7]

▌ Silence
(15–20 minutes)

▌ Rest and Journaling
(5–10 minutes)

Ask the participants to record in their journals any thoughts and images they had during the silence.

❚ Reflection Questions
(5–10 minutes)

Ask the participants to ponder the following questions and respond to them in their journals.

1. What is it like to be known by God?
2. What word or phrase, if any, became central for you?

❚ Small Group Sharing
(10–15 minutes)

Ask the participants to share their responses in pairs or small groups.

❚ Plenary
(5–15 minutes)

Ask the participants to share an insight they learned from the small group sharing.

❚ Closing Prayer Circle
(5–10 minutes)

Ask the participants to gather in a circle for prayer. Refer to page 41 for suggestions.

❚ Homework

Ask the participants to do the same exercise at home with Psalm 63. Write on newsprint the following instructions while you cite them aloud.

Read the passage twice.
Reflect on a phrase or word that "shimmers" for you.
After your silence, write in your journal about your desire for God's presence and your sense of God's desire for you.

Suggestions for Further Reading

1. John Powell, S.J., *Unconditional Love: Love without Limits*. Copyright © 1978 by Tabor Publishing (Allen, TX: Tabor Communications, 1978). The story of Tommy poignantly describes an unsuccessful search for God and then being found by God.

2. Francis Thompson, "The Hound of Heaven," reprinted in *I Fled Him, down the nights and down the days*, with photographic commentary by Algimantas Kezys, S.J., and the text with interpretive commentary and annotations by John J. Quinn, S.J. Copyright © 1970 Loyola University Press. This is a classic poem about God's seeking us.

3. The hymn "I Sought the Lord" (text written anonymously in 1890).
This hymn describes God's initiative, not ours:

I sought the Lord, and afterward I knew
He moved my soul to seek him,
    seeking me;
It was not I that found, O Saviour true;
No, I was found of thee.

Thou didst reach forth Thy hand and
    mine enfold;
I walked and sank not on the storm-
    vexed sea;
'Twas not so much that I on Thee took
    hold,
As Thou, dear Lord, on me.

I find, I walk, I love, but O, the whole
Of love is but my answer, Lord, to
    Thee;
For Thou wert long beforehand with
    my soul;
Always thou lovedst me.

Model

C

■ **Psalm 23**

■ **Guided Relaxation/
Body Prayer**
(5–10 minutes)

See pages 22–26 for suggestions.

■ **Brief Presentation**
(10–15 minutes)

Note: If this is the first time for using Scripture, please begin with "An Introduction to Praying with Scripture" (pages 44–45).

Read aloud the following or state in your own words.

Along with the Lord's Prayer, this is the best-known passage in the Bible. It has a brief simplicity. The imagery brings comfort and is realistic to behold. It enables one to see life as a whole, not just a fragment.

Although it expressed the feelings of Judeans during the Babylonian exile, it still can express our feelings and faith today.

Directions

(*Choose one of the following.*)
1. Read Psalm 23 twice from the King James Version with pauses in between. Or you might want to read it once from the King James Version and once from another version.

2. Play a musical version of Psalm 23 for a quiet meditation such as the following:

"Psalm 23," from *Come to the Quiet*, by John Michael Talbot.[8]

"Psalm 23: The Lord Is My Shepherd," from *The Gelineau Psalms*, performed by the Choir of The Cathedral Church of St. Mary, Edinburgh.[9] (Words may be found in Retreat Theme 1. Simple Gifts, page 102.)

(If people are attracted to the different words, be prepared to have a handout ready at the end of the time together, but not while they are listening and in silence. It tends to draw one away from attentiveness and openness.)

■ **Silence**
(15–20 minutes)

■ **Rest and Journaling**
(5–10 minutes)

Ask the participants to record in their journals any thoughts and images they had during the above experience.

▌ Reflection Questions
(5–10 minutes)

Ask the participants to ponder the following questions and respond to them in their journals.

1. Was there a particular line or phrase that you felt drawn toward? If so, describe it.
2. Was there a feeling or an emotion that was called forth in you? If so, describe it.
3. Do you feel that the psalm calls for any response? If so, describe it.

▌ Small Group Sharing
(10–15 minutes)

Ask the participants to share their responses in pairs or small groups.

▌ Plenary
(5–15 minutes)

Ask the participants to share any insight they learned from the small group sharing.

▌ Closing Prayer Circle
(5–10 minutes)

Ask the participants to gather in a circle for prayer. After intercessory prayer, go around the circle saying to the person next to you, "[*Name*], may God lead you beside restful waters."

▌ Homework

Ask the participants to do one of the following.

1. This week write in your journals about some of the "darkest valleys" you have felt lately—fears, hostile feelings, hurts, and so forth. Ask God to reveal these, and then use the phrase: "I fear no evil; for you are with me."
2. Write a response to the following questions in your journal:

   ▪ When have you recently found life to be most satisfying? When have your relationships with others and with God been good?

   ▪ Ask God to help you be aware of these happy and peaceful times, then respond with these words: "Surely goodness and kindness shall follow me all the days of my life."

Model

D

▌Foot Washing

▌ Guided Relaxation/ Body Prayer
(5–10 minutes)

See pages 22–26 for suggestions.

▌ Brief Presentation
(10–15 minutes)

Setting

Basin, pitcher filled with water, and a towel on floor in center of circle.

Distribute copies of the picture of "Christ Washing Peter's Feet," by Ford Madox Brown, found on page 53.

Read aloud John 13:3–9, 12–16.

Have a pitcher with water in it, ready to pour into a large basin.

Background on Scripture Reading

Read aloud the following or state in your own words.

It was the social custom for visitors after a long journey to be taken to a room where a bath was prepared. If they had come only a short distance, the slave unfastened their sandals and carried the shoes away. Then the slave would wash their feet as they reclined at the table.

In the passage we just read, the menial act of foot washing takes place during supper. Prior to this, the disciples had argued about who would be first in the kingdom and who would sit where, so they were not about to get up and play the slave's part. At this point Jesus stood up and performed this menial task, then resumed his place at the table.

In the part where Peter protests, the pronouns are most emphatic in the Greek. "Lord, are *you* going to wash *my* feet?" Jesus replies, "You do not know now what I am doing, but later you will understand" (vs. 6–7). Although there are a number of symbolic interpretations, this clearly is an act of service and an example of humility, the kind of action to which we are all called.

(Choose one of the two selections on pages 50–51 to process with the participants.)

"God in an Apron"*

When he had washed their feet and put on his outer garments again he went back to the table. "Do you understand," he said, "what I have done to you? You call me Master and Lord, and rightly; so I am. If I, then, the Lord and Master, have washed your feet, you must wash each other's feet."

(*John 13:1–14*)

Try to imagine this scene. You are sitting at the table with Jesus and his friends on the night before he died. A confusing sorrow overshadows you. Yet, a mysterious hope has settled in your heart. Suddenly Jesus is standing in front of you. He looks into your eyes and immediately you are filled with an awareness of your tremendous worth.

Supper was special that night
There was both a heaviness and a holiness
    hanging in the air
We couldn't explain the mood
It was sacred, yet sorrowful.
Gathered around that table
    eating that solemn, holy meal
    seemed to us the most important meal
    we had ever sat down to eat.

We were dwelling in the heart of *mystery*
Though dark the night
Hope felt right
    as if something evil
    was about to be conquered.

And then suddenly
the One we loved startled us all
He got up from the table
and put on an apron.
Can you imagine how we felt?
God in an apron!

Tenderness encircled us
    as He bowed before us.
He knelt and said,
    "I choose to wash your feet
    because I love you."

God in an apron, kneeling
I couldn't believe my eyes.
I was embarrassed
    until his eyes met mine
I sensed my value then.
He touched my feet
He held them in his strong, brown hands
He washed them
I can still feel the water
I can still feel the touch of his hands.
I can still see the look in his eyes.

Then he handed me the towel
    and said,
"As I have done
so you must do."
Learn to bow
Learn to kneel.

Let your tenderness encircle
    everyone you meet
Wash their feet
    not because *you have to,*
    because *you want to.*

It seems I've stood two thousand years
    holding the towel in my hands,
"As I have done so you must do,"
    keeps echoing in my heart.

"There are so many feet to wash,"
    I keep saying.
"No," I hear God's voice
    resounding through the years
"There are only my feet
What you do for them
    you do for me."

*"God in an Apron," from *Seasons of Your Heart: Prayers and Reflections*, by Macrina Wiederkehr, pp. 78–80. Copyright © 1991 by Macrina Wiederkehr. Reprinted by permission of HarperCollins Publishers, Inc.

"Would You Mind If I Wash Your Feet?"*

If Christ should suddenly stand before me with a towel thrown over his shoulder and a pan of water in his hands, would I have the humility to take off my shoes and really let him wash my feet? Or, like Peter, would I say: "What, my feet, Lord? Never!"

Christ has stood in front of me on many a day. It hasn't always been a pan of water that he's held in front of me, for water is only one symbol of a way to be cleansed and healed. Sometimes he holds a Bible, or sends a letter, or calls me on the telephone. Sometimes she holds a loaf of bread, or a cup of tea, or gives me her shoulder to cry on. Christ comes in so many ways, in so many people, always holding out that basin of water and asking that same embarrassing question: "Would you mind if I wash your feet?"

The beautiful thing about that burning, persistent, footwashing question is that eventually it calls forth the same question from your heart. Then you discover that your basin is full of water and your heart is full of a call: a call to wash feet.

*"Would You Mind If I Wash Your Feet?" from *Seasons of Your Heart: Prayers and Reflections*, by Macrina Wiederkehr, p. 80. Copyright © 1991 by Macrina Wiederkehr. Reprinted by permission of HarperCollins Publishers, Inc.

Directions

Read aloud the following to the participants.

Give yourself permission—no expectations—during silence, be gentle with yourself, and come back without any judgment.

Close your eyes. Get comfortable.

You are at the table with the disciples and Jesus in the Upper Room. You will be Peter.

During supper, Jesus, well aware that the Almighty One had entrusted everything to him and that he had come from God and was going back to God, gets up from the table, lays aside his garments, and takes a towel, tying it around himself. He then pours water into a basin (*pour water*) and begins to wash the disciples' feet and wipes them with the towel.

Now it is your turn. You are alone with Jesus in the room.

Take off your shoes and socks (or picture yourself doing so) and then allow Jesus to wash your feet. Experience that moment during our period of silence.

❚ Silence
(15–20 minutes)

▌ Rest and Journaling
(5–10 minutes)

Ask the participants to record in their journals any thoughts or images they had during the silence.

▌ Reflection Questions
(5–10 minutes)

Ask the participants to ponder the following questions and respond to them in their journals.

1. What feelings did you notice when meeting Jesus? Was there any resistance?
2. What did you learn about yourself? about God?
3. What happened in your quiet time, if anything, that assisted you in noticing God's presence? or lack of presence?

▌ Small Group Sharing
(10–15 minutes)

Ask the participants to share their responses in pairs or small groups.

▌ Plenary
(5–15 minutes)

Ask the participants to share an insight that they learned from the small group sharing.

▌ Closing Prayer Circle
(5–10 minutes)

Ask the participants to gather in a circle for prayer. Refer to page 41 for suggestions.

▌ Optional Experience

Depending on the size of the group, and the participants' relative comfort level or degree of openness, you might actually go around and wash each person's feet. If it is part of a series, they could be told to wear socks. If they would not be comfortable with this, you might have them take off their shoes and then do a simple massage over their socks, symbolically "wiping" them with the towel.

"CHRIST WASHING PETER'S FEET," BY FORD MADOX BROWN

Model

E

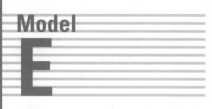

▌ The Aramaic Lord's Prayer

▌ Guided Relaxation/ Body Prayer
(5–10 minutes)

See pages 22–26 for suggestions.

▌ Brief Presentation
(10–15 minutes)

Read aloud Matt. 6:5–15 or Luke 11:1–13. Then read aloud the following background material or state in your own words.

The Lord's Prayer has been called a catechism on prayer. Taking Jesus' words from Matthew and Luke, it was used for the instruction of the newly baptized. The Matthew passage was addressed to the Jewish Christians who knew about praying since childhood, and the Luke passage was for Gentile Christians who were learning to pray for the first time. It is felt that the Luke version is probably the oldest form and that Matthew incorporates liturgical forms. The original language was Aramaic. Prayer in Jesus' name began with the Lord's Prayer. Addressing God as "Abba" was a new, personal approach. No Jew would have dared to address God as such. The word used by Jesus implied an intimate family relationship. While a rabbi might have used it with the translation "Our

Father," no Jew would have said, "My Father."

Directions

Distribute the Lord's Prayer in Aramaic with the translation found on page 56. Review the English; repeat together once. Then go over the Aramaic and repeat line by line. After everyone is comfortable with the words, explain that they will begin to repeat the lines without stopping. This is a chant. Prior to beginning the chant, say this:

> Feel it . . . the sounds . . . the rhythm . . . the rhyme.
> Let it sink in . . . from your vocal cords to your inner being.
> Be with the disciples, learning it together.
> *(Begin the chant in Aramaic.)*

▌ Silence
(15–20 minutes)

▌ Rest and Journaling
(5–10 minutes)

Ask the participants to record in their journals any thoughts or images they had during the silence.

▌ Reflection Questions
(5–10 minutes)

Ask the participants to ponder the following questions and respond to them in their journals.

1. Reflect on what sort of a relationship you have with the Lord's Prayer.
2. What does it mean to you today?
3. Are there any parts that speak to you in a special way? Are there any parts that make you feel uncomfortable?

▌ Small Group Sharing
(10–15 minutes)

Ask the participants to share their responses in pairs or small groups.

▌ Plenary
(5–15 minutes)

Ask the participants to share an insight they learned from the small group sharing.

▌ Closing Prayer Circle
(5–10 minutes)

Ask the participants to gather in a circle for prayer. Refer to page 41 for suggestions.

The Lord's Prayer, Approximate Aramaic Translation*

(Vowels are soft except as marked: ch has a k sound as in Hebrew or German; the accent is always on the last syllable as marked.)

ABBÁ	Dear Father
YITHKADUSH SHEMACH	Holy Be Your Name
TĀYTHĀY MALKUTHACH	Let Come Your Kingdom
LACHMAN d'LIMHAR	Our Bread For Tomorrow
HABLUN YOMAd'HEN	Give Us Today
USHBAKLAN CHOBĀNE	Forgive Us Our Offenses
k'DISHBAKNAN l'CHAYYABHĀNE	For We Also Forgive Our Debtors
ŪHLÁ THALINAN l'NISYŌN	And Let Not Us Fall Into Temptation

Joachim Jeremias in *The Prayers of Jesus* says one "can easily spot the characteristic features of this solemn language. We should note three features especially [of the Aramaic]: parallelism, the two-beat rhythm, and the rhyme in lines two and four, which is scarcely accidental. The Lord's Prayer in Jesus' tongue sounded something like this (the accents designate the two-beat rhythm).

'Abbá'
yithquaddásh sh°mákh / tethé
    malkhuthákh
lahmán d°limhár / habh lán yoma
    dhén
ushbhoq lán hobhaín /
    k°dhish°bháqnan l°hayyabhaín
w°la thaelínnan l°nisyón."**

---

*This version was used by Gerald May in a ten-week Shalem program on "Historical Holiness," October 9, 1985, as it appeared in Joachim Jeremias, *The Prayers of Jesus* (Naperville, IL: Alec R. Allenson, 1967). Reprinted from *The Lord's Prayer,* by Joachim Jeremias, translated by John Reumann, pp. 93–94. Copyright © 1964 Fortress Press. Used by permission of Augsburg Fortress.

**Reprinted from *The Lords' Prayer*, by Joachim Jeremias, translated by John Reumann, pp. 93–94. Copyright © 1964 Fortress Press. Used by permission of Augsburg Fortress. A recent interesting and usable source on this subject is *Prayers of the Cosmos: Meditations on the Aramaic Words of Jesus*, translated with commentary by Neil Douglas-Klotz; foreword by Matthew Fox. It refers to the work of Dr. George M. Lamsa, the pioneering Aramaic scholar of the 1930s whose scholarly book, *The New Testament According to the Eastern Text* (Philadelphia: A. J. Holman, 1940), translated from original Aramaic Sources, may still be found in libraries.

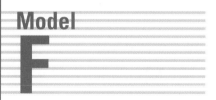

Model F

▋ Bar-timaeus/ Bat-timaeus

▋ **Guided Relaxation/ Body Prayer**
(5–10 minutes)

See pages 22–26 for suggestions.

▋ **Brief Presentation**
(10–15 minutes)

Directions

We will use a Gospel story to hear God's word for us today. Through our memory, as well as our imagination, we will let the past become the present. We want to let our whole being be open to Christ working through the events of the passage.

Put yourself in the picture, in the scene, as gently as you can. Don't work at it. Just allow yourself to be present with the characters along the dusty road, noticing any sights or smells or sounds that might be present. If you can't "image" easily, then just "sense" the scene.

The passage will be read twice. When the passage is completed, let the scene fade; simply be present with Jesus.

Read Mark 10:46 first as Bar-timaeus, then as Bat-timaeus.[10] *Bar-timaeus* means "son of Timaeus"; *Bat-timaeus* means "daughter of Timaeus."

▋ **Silence**
(15–20 minutes)

▋ **Rest and Journaling**
(5–10 minutes)

Read aloud the following or state in your own words.

Let yourself dialogue with Jesus now in writing. Begin a script that has Jesus saying: "[*Your name*], what do you want me to do for you?" Then you respond. You may want to ask something. You may be spoken to. You may want to reply or perhaps be silent. Let it evolve as God wills. If you experience discomfort or other emotions, share that with Jesus. Be as open and receptive as you can in your conversation.

▌ Reflection Questions
(5–10 minutes)

Choose two of the following questions and ask the participants to ponder them and respond to them in their journals.

1. Did this experience assist you in being present and perhaps open to God? How?
2. Were there any moments of grace? When?
3. Were you resistant or reluctant to meet Jesus personally? Was that resolved in any way?
4. Did this connect with what's going on in your life with God now? How?

▌ Small Group Sharing
(10–15 minutes)

Ask the participants to share their responses in pairs or small groups.

▌ Plenary
(5–15 minutes)

Ask the participants to share an insight they learned from the small group sharing.

▌ Closing Prayer Circle
(5–10 minutes)

Ask the participants to gather in a circle for prayer. Refer to page 41 for suggestions.

▌ Homework

Choose another Gospel passage where you can "put yourself in the picture" and sit with it. (Examples may be the rich young ruler, Zacchaeus, the prodigal son, or Mary and Martha.) Be silent, reflect, and absorb the whole scene. Dialogue or write in your journal about your time together with the character from this Scripture.

Model

G

∎ The Jesus Prayer

∎ Guided Relaxation/ Body Prayer
(5–10 minutes)

See pages 22–26 for suggestions.

∎ Brief Presentation
(10–15 minutes)

Write The Jesus Prayer on chalkboard or newsprint:

> "Lord Jesus Christ, [Son of God], have mercy on me, [a sinner]."

Background on Scripture Reading

Read aloud the following or state in your own words.

This verse is known as "The Jesus Prayer." The words in the brackets were not always part of the prayer, especially the last phrase, "a sinner."

The prayer's origins date back to the sixth century to the monastery of St. Catherine on Mount Sinai. In the fourteenth century, Gregory of Sinai brought it to Mount Athos in Macedonia. In the eighteenth century, many peoples' experiences were written down and published in a book still available today called *The Philokalia*,[11] which means "the love of the beautiful"; namely, the splendor of the realm of God. A decade later it was translated from Greek into Russian and is mostly known to us through the nineteenth-century story of a Russian peasant's pilgrimage, *The Way of a Pilgrim*,[12] which was translated into English in the twentieth century. The peasant seeks to find a way in which he can observe the exhortation found in 1 Thess. 5:17: "pray without ceasing." The Jesus Prayer can also be found in J. D. Salinger's novel *Franny and Zooey*, in which a schoolgirl discovers the practice and tries to apply it to her unstable, confused existence.

Many books have since been written to either describe the practice, to give its history, or to make it applicable for today. It is described in Ira Progoff's *The Practice of Process Meditation*,[13] used as a meditation form in John Westerhoff's book *Inner Growth/Outer Change*,[14] and is covered in its entirety very nicely in a small volume by Per-Olof Sjögren titled *The Jesus Prayer*.[15]

This prayer is also called "The Prayer of the Heart," since it does not involve the intellect. No effort needs to be made by the mind or the will; nor is one in control of anything. It prays itself, as the saying goes.

In *The Way of a Pilgrim*, the peasant realizes that his mind is not

enough to achieve the answer he seeks. His joy with the newfound technique from *The Philokalia* is described as "a most delightful warmth, as well as consolation and peace."[16]

It has been called the perfect prayer. The oldest part is "Have mercy on me," an Old Testament cry to God. We hear those words used in the New Testament by Bartimaeus, the Canaanite woman, the ten lepers, and the publican—all ask Jesus to have mercy on them.

In the early church, the first affirmation that was used to express personal commitment was "Jesus is Lord," which became a later addition to the prayer. This was intended to invoke Christ's presence, much as the word "Jahweh" was spoken once a year in the Holy of Holies. The name of Jesus continued to be used as an invocation, and by the sixth century it appeared in the liturgy with the added phrase "Lord, have mercy" (the Kyrie Eleison) as a congregational response during the Eucharist.

Some benefits from using The Jesus Prayer are as follows:

■ It can silence our egos and help to diminish our preoccupation with thoughts and feelings that draw us away from our desire for God.

■ Since part of its story is rooted in praying without ceasing (see 1 Thess. 5:17 and Phil. 2:9–11), it may draw us toward reading the Bible.

■ It can be prayed at any time, even in the midst of busyness.

Directions

The instructions that were given to the pilgrim were these:

> Sit down alone and in silence. Lower your head, shut your eyes, breathe out gently and imagine yourself looking into your own heart. Carry your mind, that is, your thoughts, from your head to your heart. As you breathe out, say "Lord Jesus Christ, have mercy on me." Say it moving your lips gently, or simply say it in your mind. Try to put all other thoughts aside. Be calm, be patient, and repeat the phrase very frequently.[17]

Alternative Directions

Close your eyes and get comfortable. Have both feet flat on the floor and your back straight to assist in attentiveness. Let your hands rest in your lap, palms upward and open. Be conscious of becoming still. Gently let thoughts go. Be aware of your breathing as it slows down. Rest in that silence for a few minutes. Now, as you inhale, say to yourself: "Lord Jesus Christ" and as you exhale: "Have mercy on me" (or "Have mercy on me, a sinner"; if you use this version it might help to understand "sinner" as one who has been separated from God).

Continue to repeat this over and over until you hear the sound of the bell.

▌ Silence
(15–20 minutes)

▌ Rest and Journaling
(5–10 minutes)

Ask the participants to record in their journals any thoughts or images they had during the silence.

▌ Reflection Questions
(5–10 minutes)

Ask the participants to ponder the following questions and respond to them in their journals.

1. What is it like to ask for God's mercy? to receive God's mercy?
2. What is it like for you to repeatedly call on Christ?

▌ Small Group Sharing
(10–15 minutes)

Ask the participants to share their responses in pairs or small groups.

▌ Plenary
(5–15 minutes)

Ask the participants to share an insight they learned from the small group sharing.

▌ Closing Prayer Circle
(5–10 minutes)

Ask the participants to gather in a circle for prayer. Refer to page 41 for suggestions.

▌ Homework

Practice the prayer during the week, not just in your quiet time, but when you go through your day. When you are tempted to say something inspired by ego defensiveness or aggression, take a breath and think, "Lord, have mercy . . . give them what they need" or whatever seems appropriate.[18]

Model
H

▌ "Stay Here and Watch with Me"

▌ Guided Relaxation/ Body Prayer
(5–10 minutes)

See pages 22–26 for suggestions.

▌ Brief Presentation
(10–15 minutes)

Read aloud Mark 14:32–38 or Matt. 26:36–41. Then read aloud the following background material or state in your own words.

The disciples, at a crucial time, had some difficulty "watching and praying." They fell asleep. We, too, may have difficulty with this discipline. Yet we can practice it—not only for the crucial times of life, but as a way of becoming more responsive to God's Spirit every day.

The Greek word in the New Testament translated as "watch" means "to stay awake" and "to be attentive." Watching is an important corollary of praying. It is the discipline of staying awake and alert; it is being attentive to what is going on around and within. Watching opens the senses, sharpens the attention, and clears the way for prayer.

Directions

Our acquaintance with Scripture may cause us to read familiar words and miss the Word meant for us. The repetition of a phrase can allow the Word to gradually sink into our hearts until we feel it at work within us. This may be experienced in any number of ways. Music is able to touch the depths of our souls as well as to help keep us focused. In a group setting, chanting can help in evoking this awareness. We can also participate vicariously by listening to others chant. The repetition serves to reinforce the words in our hearts, leading us to hear them more personally.

Play the chant, "Stay Here," from the Taizé tape or compact disc *Laudate*.[19] (10 minutes)

Alternative Directions

Acquaint the group with the tune (from a Taizé songbook or the tape), but sing the chant as a group rather than just listening to it. Another possibility that has been used successfully is to listen to the piece, then chant it as a group for about four minutes before the silence. Hearing the chant brings one into the scene; personal involvement makes one a participant in it.

▌ Silence
(15–20 minutes)

▌ Rest and Journaling
(5–10 minutes)

Ask the participants to record in their journals any thoughts or images they had during the silence.

▌ Reflection Questions
(5–10 minutes)

Ask the participants to ponder the following questions and respond to them in their journals.

1. What happened to your desire and presence for God in your prayer time?
2. Did you notice any resistance or distractions? (Affirm naturalness of dis-ease. We're all resisters, and we're physically and neurologically distracted too.)
3. Was there anything God seemed to be asking of you? If so, how did you respond?

▌ Small Group Sharing
(10–15 minutes)

Ask the participants to share their responses in pairs or small groups.

▌ Plenary
(5–15 minutes)

Ask the participants to share an insight they learned from the small group sharing.

▌ Closing Prayer Circle
(5–10 minutes)

Ask the participants to gather in a circle for prayer. Refer to page 41 for suggestions.

▌ Homework

1. Sing through "Jesus, Remember Me"[20] (from Taizé music tape or compact disc *Laudate*), so that it is familiar and easy to repeat, even in relative silence at home. Write in your journal about how God seemed to be present (or not) through sound and through word.

2. Have samples of Taizé tapes and Shalem tapes available should people wish to use them.

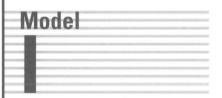

Model

▌ The Rich Young Ruler

▌ Guided Relaxation/ Body Prayer
(5–10 minutes)

See pages 22–26 for suggestions.

▌ Brief Presentation
(10–15 minutes)

Read aloud the following or state in your own words.

Stories from Scripture are often read as other peoples' stories, not anything remotely close to our circumstances. Getting "into" the story sometimes helps to bring it closer to our hearts where we can deal with it.

Directions

Read Mark 10:17–22. Ask the participants to picture the scene as if they were there. "You see Jesus. What is your hope?"

Then reread the passage, asking the participants to place themselves in the story. Pause occasionally so that the participants can experience a moment of silence, then conclude the Scripture reading. Ask participants to remain silent and sit quietly without searching or censoring. Have them focus on being alone with Jesus—asking questions and listening attentively to what may come. Then say the following:

As Jesus is setting out on a journey, you run up to him and kneel before him, and ask, "Good Teacher, what must I do to inherit eternal life?" Jesus says to you, "Why do you call me good? No one is good but God alone. You know the commandments: 'You shall not murder; You shall not commit adultery; You shall not steal; You shall not bear false witness; You shall not defraud; Honor your father and mother.'" You say to him, "Teacher, I have kept all these since my youth." Jesus looks at you, loves you, and says, "You lack one thing: _____." (*Pause; short period of silence.*) When you hear this, you are shocked and go away grieving.

▌ Silence
(15–20 minutes)

▌ Rest and Journaling
(5–10 minutes)

Ask the participants to record in their journals any thoughts or images they had during the silence.

▌ Reflection Questions
(5–10 minutes)

Ask the participants to ponder the following questions and respond to them in their journals.

1. What was it like to be alone with Jesus?
2. How did you feel when Jesus told you that you lacked one thing?
3. What resistance, if any, did you experience when you heard the story told this way?
4. Were you helped in any way to get in touch with a stumbling block that might be present in your relationship with God? How?

▌ Small Group Sharing
(10–15 minutes)

Ask the participants to share their responses in pairs or small groups.

▌ Plenary
(5–15 minutes)

Ask the participants to share an insight they learned from the small group sharing.

▌ Closing Prayer Circle
(5–10 minutes)

Ask the participants to gather in a circle for prayer. Refer to page 41 for suggestions.

Model
J

▮ Meditation on Water

▮ Guided Relaxation/ Body Prayer
(5–10 minutes)

Begin with some opening movements from pages 22–26, then ask the participants to do the following:

Move as though you are walking slowly to the water's edge. Walk into the water. Lift your hands to your waist. Lie down. Let the water surround you, wash over you, calm you. Place your arms over your head, relaxed into a sign of openness, of blessing.

Now place your arms by your sides. Relinquish and let yourself be carried by the water.

Wiggle your toes. Know that you are alive. Feel life moving up in your body.

Breathe deeply. You have received the breath of life and become a living soul!

▮ Brief Presentation
(10–15 minutes)

Have a large scallop shell for the central focus and a smaller one for each person. *Read aloud the following or state in your own words.*

Our dependency on our eyes to process what is "out there" can be both a help and a hindrance. Too often we see something and immediately label and judge it, thereby preventing us from seeing its value as a source of learning. On the other hand, if we remember that the eyes are "the window of the soul," and allow ourselves to separate from that need to analyze, we can be innocently present in whatever we behold. This is like having the eyes of a child, accepting the realm of God as a child (Mark 10:15) or humbling oneself like a child (Matt. 18:4)—all indicating innocence and simplicity. As adults culturally trained in rather opposing viewpoints, we do not find it easy to let go of mental assessments and interpretations. We do tend to believe, however, that God is all and in all. So perhaps we can affirm that truth as we behold all things, being intentional about our desire to be totally present before and between our thoughts arising.

Directions

Give each person a scallop shell (baptismal shell) and pour a tad of water in each one. *Read aloud John 4:13–14. Read aloud the following or state in your own words.*

Let yourself be known by God through the water. Touch it, feel it, stare at it, focus on it, be with it without "thinking" about it. If at any time you want to set it down, feel free to do so. Let the water become a window to God for you in this silence.

▌ Silence
(15–20 minutes)

▌ Rest and Journaling
(5–10 minutes)

Ask the participants to continue in the silence and express this experience in their journals with crayons and paper in any way that seems appropriate.

▌ Reflection Questions
(5–10 minutes)

Ask the participants to ponder the following questions and respond to them in their journals.

1. Did the water assist you in your presence for God? How?
2. Did you find yourself eager and trusting or fearful and resistant? Did you feel free to be vulnerably present for God? Or were you fearful and perhaps resistant, distancing yourself by stepping "outside" to "think" about it?

▌ Small Group Sharing
(10–15 minutes)

Ask the participants to share their responses in pairs or small groups.

▌ Plenary
(5–15 minutes)

Ask the participants to share an insight they learned from the small group sharing.

▌ Closing Prayer Circle
(5–10 minutes)

Ask the participants to gather in a circle for prayer. Refer to page 41 for suggestions.

▌ Homework

Sit before an object in the same way in your quiet place. You might want to use a candle, a rock or stone or precious gem, a cross, a twig, or a bowl. Focus on it. Let God meet you before, through, and after your thoughts. Write in your journal about the experience.

Alternative Directions

Give each person a scallop shell. Read the following Scriptures, showing slides or pictures if possible to illustrate each.

> Save me, O God;
> for the waters have come up to
> my neck.
> I sink in deep mire,
> where there is no foothold;
> I have come into deep waters,
> and the flood sweeps over me.
> (Ps. 69:1–2)

> Do not fear, for I have redeemed
> you;
> I have called you by name, you
> are mine.
> When you pass through the waters,
> I will be with you;
> and through the rivers, they
> shall not overwhelm you.
> (Isa. 43:1b–2)

> Let the sea roar, and all that fills it;
> the world and those who live in
> it.
> Let the floods clap their hands;
> let the hills sing together for
> joy . . .
> (Ps. 98:7–8)

> Jesus said to her, "Everyone who drinks of this water will be thirsty again, but those who drink of the water that I will give them will never be thirsty. The water that I will give will become in them a spring of water gushing up to eternal life."
> (John 4:13–14)

The biblical references to water range from creation to ordinary usage. References to water appear in miracles as well as in the judgment (the flood).

Water can calm, it can cleanse, it can destroy.

Recall times in your life when water calmed you, when it cleansed you, or when it endangered you.

(*Pour water into each person's shell*.)

Look steadily at the water. Put your fingers in it and let them rest in it.

Allow your own memories of water to flow back to the times

when it has affected you . . .
when it has made you happy . . .
when it has threatened you . . .
when it has served you . . .

Be with the water and let it speak to you in the silence. If you wish to put the shell down during the silence, feel free to do so.

Teresa of Avila said that water is used "to convey the sense of hidden riches and depths within the human person. [It represents an] awareness of the deep, interior presence of God."[21]

Carl Jung said, "Whenever water appears it is usually the water of life, meaning a medium through which one is reborn. It symbolizes a sort of baptism ceremony, or initiation, a healing bath that gives resurrection or rebirth."[22]

Distribute copies of the text of "Blessing of the Easter Water" (page 69), by the Monks of Weston Priory for the participants to follow along as the tape is played.

Play the tape.

Silence
(15 to 20 minutes)

Rest and Journaling
(5–10 minutes)

Ask the participants to record in their journals any thoughts or images they had during the silence.

▌ Reflection Questions
(5–10 minutes)

Ask the participants to ponder the following questions and respond to them in their journals.

1. How is God present for you in water?
2. How is God present for you through your experience of water?
3. How is God present for you through your longing for water or fear of water?

▌ Small Group Sharing
(10–15 minutes)

Ask the participants to discuss in pairs or small groups the following questions.

1. Did any of these questions, quotations, Scripture passages, songs, or the water itself speak to you in a special way?
2. Did they trigger anything?

▌ Closing Prayer Circle
(5–10 minutes)

Ask the participants to gather in a circle for prayer, asking them to give thanks for one of the ways God is present for them in water.

Blessing of the Easter Water*

Weston Priory
Gregory Norbet OSB

(*with sounds of water being poured*)

Leader:
Brothers and sisters:
*Let us ask the Lord our God
to breathe his restless Spirit
upon this water,
gift of his hand,
and sign of our baptism,
and upon us,
that we may be faithful
to the new life we have
received.*

Chorus:
*O, come to the waters,
You who thirst, come to me.
Listen, listen, and you shall live.*

Leader:
**We praise you, our creating
God,**
*for fresh water,
sparkling mirror of your glory;
for humble water,
out of which life first sprang,
and upon which
the first path to new life
was charted;
for the parting waters of Exodus,
clearing freedom's highway
out of the house of slavery;
for the waters of repentance,
flowing straight into the hearts
of your people
at the word of John the
Baptist;
for the Living Water, your Son,
pouring himself out like a
flood,
quenching our thirst with his
love.*

Chorus:
*O, come to the waters,
You who thirst, come to me,
Listen, listen, and you shall live.*

Leader:
God,
*take this our water,
once more as your own.
Make it really alive,
as in the beginning;
You who are Creator,
brood over it in love
as tender Mother,
And fashion us anew
in the image of Jesus
who is alive for ever.*

Chorus:
*O, come to the waters,
You who thirst, come to me.
Listen, listen, and you shall live.*

*Copyright © 1982, from the recording *Easter Blessings and Promises*, The Benedictine Foundation of the State of Vermont, Inc., Weston Priory, Weston, VT 05161. Used by permission.

Model K

A Meditation on Hands

Guided Relaxation/ Body Prayer
(5–10 minutes)

See pages 22–26 for suggestions.

Brief Presentation
(10–15 minutes)

1. Read some Scripture passages that mention the hand. For example:

> . . . The LORD your God will bless you in all your produce and in all the work of your hands, so that you will be altogether joyful.
>> (Deut. 16:15, RSV)

> Let the favor of the Lord our God be upon us,
> and prosper for us the work of our hands
> O prosper the work of our hands!
>> (Ps. 90:17)

> The eye cannot say to the hand, "I have no need of you."
>> (1 Cor. 12:21)

2. Say the following prayer, or one of your own:

> I am so afraid to open my clenched fists!
> Who will I be when I have nothing left to hold on to?
> Who will I be when I stand before you with empty hands?
> Please help me to gradually open my hands
> and to discover that I am not what I own,
> but what you want to give me.
> And what you want to give me is love,
> unconditional, everlasting love.[23]

Directions

See that people are sitting in a circle where they will be able to touch one another without reaching too far. However, it is important not to reveal at this time that they will be touching. Read the following hand meditation very slowly.

Get comfortable. Be aware of your body and your breath. Gradually notice your breathing as it becomes slower. Close your eyes, if they are not already closed. Relax any tension points and appreciate the stillness.

Very gently move your hands and fingers like the opening of flower petals so that your hands come to rest on your lap, palms facing upward. Notice the sensation in the palms, the gesture it might represent to you. Become aware of the air at your fingertips, between your fingers, and on the palm of your hand. Experience the fullness, strength, and maturity of your hands.

Reflect on *your* hands. Then become aware of the most unforgettable hands you have known. Remember the oldest hands that have rested in your hands. See the hands of a newborn child, their incredible beauty, perfection, delicacy; the soft, smooth hands of a child—once upon a time, your hands were like that.

Stretch your hands about, opening and closing them, letting those motions assist you in picturing all that your hands have done to help you learn, and love, and "be" for others. Clasp them together until you can feel the firm grip. In what ways have they reached out to help others? Feel the tiredness and aching they have known, the cold and the heat, the soreness and the bruises.

Now wipe your brow and remember the tears your hands have wiped away—your own or another's—the healing they have brought when laid gently on a hurting place.

Grasp your knees and feel the anger and violence they have expressed. Then bring them to your chest in a cradling position, and experience the gentleness, the tenderness, the love they have given. Fold them in prayer and observe how that gesture affects you.

Now raise your right hand slowly and gently place it over your heart. Press more firmly until your hand picks up the beat of your heart, that most mysterious of all human sounds.

Press more firmly for a moment and then release your hand and hold it just a fraction from your clothing. Experience the warmth between your hand and your heart. Now lower your hand to your lap very carefully as if it were carrying your heart. For it does. When you extend your hand to another, it is not just bone and skin; it is your heart. A handshake is the real heart transplant. Reflect for a moment on all the hands that have left their imprint on you. See the people who carry your handprint and bear your heartprint.

Now, without opening your eyes, extend your right hand to your neighbor's left hand. Simply hold it, and sense the history and mystery of this hand. Let your hand speak to it, and let it listen to the other. Try to express your gratitude for this hand stretched out to you. Then bring your hand back again to your lap. Experience the presence of that hand lingering upon your hand—the afterglow will fade, but the print is there forever.

Whose hand was that? It could have been any hand; it could have been God's hand. It was. God has no other hands than ours.[24]

▌ Silence
(15–20 minutes)

▌ Rest and Journaling
(5–10 minutes)

Ask the participants to record in their journals any thoughts or images they had during the silence.

▌ Reflection Questions
(5–10 minutes)

Ask the participants to ponder the following questions and respond to them in their journals.

1. In what way did the use of hands assist you or become a block for you in experiencing God's presence?
2. Did you discover any resistance associated with hands that interfered with your being present for God? What might that mean for you?

▌ Small Group Sharing
(10–15 minutes)

Ask the participants to share their responses in pairs or small groups.

▌ Plenary
(5–15 minutes)

Ask the participants to share an insight they learned from the small group sharing.

▌ Closing Prayer Circle
(5–10 minutes)

Ask the participants to gather in a circle for prayer. Distribute copies of the "Hand in Hand—A Litany," page 73. You may also use the following prayer:

> The hands of the Father uphold you
> The hands of the Saviour enfold
>   you
> The hands of the Spirit surround
>   you
> And the blessing of God Almighty
> Father, Son and Holy Spirit
> Uphold you evermore. Amen.[25]

▌ Homework

Use the following as a breath prayer for the week: Psalm 119:109 (Knox) *"I carry my life in my hands."* Turning the palms of your hands up for breath prayer, use on inhalation *"my life"* and on exhalation *"in my hands."* (From *The Daybook*, a contemplative journal by Marv and Nancy Hile. Used by permission of the authors.)

Hand in Hand—A Litany*

All: Lord, here are our hands:

Left: Put in deep pockets to keep them safe.

Right: Held behind our backs to keep them hidden from you.

Left: Placed over our eyes to blind ourselves to the needs of others.

Right: Buried within sand where they are immobilized and useless.

Left: Patting ourselves on the back to take credit for all we are and do.

Right: Grabbing for the material things of life.

All: Forever pushing you away.

All: Lord, here are your hands:

Left: Tireless and always there for us.

Right: Beckoning us to come closer.

Left: Holding us secure.

Right: Lifting us up when we are down.

Left: Opening new doors for us.

Right: Revealing special gifts you have given us.

Left: Showing the way to eternal life.

Right: Touching us with overwhelming love.

All: We are never the same again.

All: Lord, we place our hands in yours.

Left: Take them to use as you will.

Right: No other hands can touch in quite the same way as ours.

All: Lord, hand in hand with you, we are:

Left: Reaching out in love to others,

Right: Inviting all to experience the abundant life,

All: Receiving much more that we give.

All: Lord, alone our hands are weak, but together, with yours, they are strong. Amen.

*From *Prayers for the Seasons of Life*. Copyright © 1997 by Sue Downing (Franklin, TN: Providence House Publishers, 1997). Reprinted by permission.

Model

L

▌ Sound and Silence

▌ Guided Relaxation/ Body Prayer
(10–15 minutes)

Read aloud the following or state in your own words.

Get in a standing position with arms overhead. Cross your arms over like the sweep of a giant clock hand, and then back up. Notice the rhythm. Notice the effort or the ease with which you lift or let go.

Standing or bending, with your arms relaxed, move your arms like an elephant trunk or a pendulum. Swing your arms side to side. Observe the effort needed to sustain the rhythmic motion.

Place your arms out to your sides with your palms up. Feel the air on your palms. Let the vibrations touch you and enter you. Raise your arms up in an arc. Bring them forward in a cup and place them in your heart.

Sit. Breathe slowly. Notice your breath.

▌ Brief Presentation[26]
(10–15 minutes)

Read aloud the following or state in your own words.

Every motion that springs forth from this silent life is a vibration and a creator of vibrations. The world was called into being by the Word. The Word was God. Creation might be called the sound or the vibration of God. In creation, when the vibrations are massed together, they become audible, or materialize. That's what we see or hear—it verifies our existence. Vibration is at the root of all creation. Even those things that seem lifeless, dead, and inanimate have vibrations. These vibrations could be a collection of atoms as in a door or a table—or a collection of sounds that might come from waterfalls, or birds or crickets, or musical instruments like percussion or brass or strings.

Normally our minds divide us from sound because we tend to label the sound. We say, "That is a cricket," and we try to grasp it. Notice what our feelings do—they judge the sound, "That is a good (or bad) sound."

Scripture acknowledges these vibrations of sound and silence. . . .

Psalm 150 (Praise the Lord with the trumpet)

Psalm 66 (Make a joyful noise to God all the earth)

Psalm 62 (For God alone my soul waits in silence)

Psalm 46 (Be still, and know that I am God)

We have a tendency to separate sound and silence, thinking they are opposite. Actually they are one. Like turning left and turning right; like God is distant and also intimate and within.

Complete or absolute silence does not exist. Even in an echoic chamber two sounds are heard: heartbeat or blood circulating and the nervous system.

Sound is a particular shaping of silence that includes all sounds. On the one hand we have a fear of being sucked into it; on the other, it is like coming home—intimate, filled with longing. Sound draws us into silence, and the silence draws us into sound. All is vibration.

In the silence, we come closer to all sounds. We begin to experience God's presence or the sense of God as the heart of sound.

Directions

Choose the following activity. You may also choose the activity on page 76.

Tibetan Singing Bells

In Tibet, a gong or a bowl or a bell (they mean the same thing) is used to assist with meditation. It is sounded at certain intervals to help the monks with their breathing and mantras. When they are well established in their practice and have achieved a correct speed—slower and slower— then the vibrations become finer and finer within the person. At this point they are better able to disregard the mind's interruptions. They establish their own reverberations.[27]

(*Go around and let each person hear the sound as you strike the side of the bell.*)

We will listen to the sound of the bells as they call us into God's presence, as they call us into the Heart of vibration, who is God. They will be struck at random in order to experience the different sounds and vibrations and to assist our attentiveness. After about ten minutes, the little bowl will be struck three times to introduce us to the fifteen to twenty minutes of silence that will follow.

▌ Silence
(15–20 minutes)

▌ Rest and Journaling
(5–10 minutes)

Ask the participants to find a comfortable position, but not one in which they find it easy to go to sleep; relaxed but attentive (alert, aware). Tell the participants that when the silence is over, the little bell will be struck again. Ask participants to rest for a few minutes and then to write anything they wish to remember in their journals.

▌ Reflection Questions
(5–10 minutes)

Choose two or three of the following questions and ask the participants to ponder them and respond to them in their journals.

1. Reflect on the time with the bells (or chant) and the time with the silence.
2. Was there a difference for you?
3. Was one experience more helpful?
4. Did one make the other more meaningful or did all merge?

5. Were you able to notice a different sense of who God is and who you are?

6. Were there any special graces you received, even if just for a few seconds?

▌ Small Group Sharing
(10–15 minutes)

Ask the participants to share their responses in pairs or small groups.

▌ Plenary
(5–15 minutes)

Ask the participants to share an insight they learned from the small group sharing.

▌ Closing Prayer Circle
(5–10 minutes)

Ask the participants to gather in a circle for prayer. Begin praying with the following:

> God, we hear you in the earthquake, wind, and fire—and in the still, small voice—that makes us aware of your presence whether in sound or silence. Hear our concerns, now both silent and spoken. . . .

▌ Homework

Be aware this week of different kinds of vibrations that you may not have recognized as such. Let sound serve as a meditation. Try not to name or judge the sounds. Be aware of sound arising out of silence and notice how much silence is retained.

Directions

Choose the following activity. You may also choose the activity appearing on page 75.

Chant

Read aloud Eph. 3:14–19. Then introduce the participants to Elizabeth of the Trinity by reading the following or stating it in your own words.

Elizabeth of the Trinity, the patron saint of spiritual guidance, lived to be only twenty-six years old (born in 1880). Her training was in the Carmelite Order and she considered her ministry to be encouraging and nurturing souls in their search for God.

Distribute the prayer on page 77 and the chant "Changeless and Calm" on page 78.

Introduce the idea of chant as a vehicle for focusing on the breath, sound, and repetition of a single concept without analysis, just letting it sink in. The group participation helps one to appreciate the practice, strange as it may seem in the beginning. Although many chants are in print and are simply passed on from one group to another, it is also possible for people to create their own. These can be single words, like "Amen," "Alleluia," or "Jahweh," or simple phrases such as "O, Holy One." Other chants are more melodic.

We will begin by listening to the chant on the tape *Sound Faith*, and gradually join in with the group as they sing it. As we grow more confident with the tune and words, the volume will be turned down until we are chanting it without accompaniment. The chant will continue for about three to five minutes; a bell will sound. (*Note*: The leader can just let the group judge when they are ready to begin silence and let it gradually soften and end, bit by bit.)

▌ Silence
(15–20 minutes)

Ask the participants to record in their journals any thoughts or images they had during the silence.

O my God, whom I adore, help me to

become wholly forgetful of self, that I may be

immovably rooted in you, as changeless and calm as

though I were already in eternity.

May nothing disturb my peace or draw me forth

from you, O my unchanging Holy One, but

may I at every moment penetrate more deeply into

the depths of your mystery.

—Elizabeth of the Trinity

Adapted by Gerald May of the Shalem Institute from a prayer of
Elizabeth of the Trinity dated November 21, 1904.

Changeless and Calm

Change - less and calm, deep mys - ter - y. E - ver more deep - ly root - ed in Thee.

God, Guide Us Home

God, guide us home, Christ, make us one;

Ho - ly Spir - it flow,_____ Love will be done.

Chants composed by Gerald May of the Shalem
Institute for Spiritual Formation. Used by permission
of the Shalem Institute.

▌Reflection Questions
(5–10 minutes)

Ask the participants to ponder the following questions and respond to them in their journals.

1. As you reflect, was the quality of consciousness when you were inside the sound different from when you were outside the sound?

2. Were you aware of any graced moments? any resistance? Can you describe it?

▌Small Group Sharing
(10–15 minutes)

Ask the participants to share their responses in pairs or small groups.

▌Plenary
(5–15 minutes)

Ask the participants to share an insight they learned from the small group sharing.

▌Closing Prayer Circle
(5–10 minutes)

The chant "God, Guide Us Home" on page 78 is excellent for closing worship at retreats or meetings. The music is pleasing to hear and sing, and the words become a benediction.

Ask the participants to gather in a circle for prayer. Play "God, Guide Us Home" and distribute copies. Ask the group to chant for approximately three to five minutes.

Model
M

▮ Seeing God in the Ordinary

▮ Guided Relaxation/ Body Prayer
(5–10 minutes)

See pages 22–26 for suggestions.

▮ Brief Presentation[28]
(10–15 minutes)

For this session, one could use any object at all: a stone, a leaf, a piece of tableware, a vase, flowers, seashells, or a window. With some imagination it is possible to see that God is everywhere and absent nowhere.

Read aloud the following or state in your own words.

Julian of Norwich was born in 1342 and apparently lived to a ripe old age. She was a hermit with profound theological insights and supernatural experiences. These events are described by Julian in her writings, *Showings*. Probably the most familiar passage is her "All shall be well, and all manner of thing shall be well."[29] She meditated on her visions for twenty years before recording them.

Directions

Give out a hazelnut to each person in the group. Then read aloud the following from Julian's writings:

> [God] showed me something small, no bigger than a hazelnut [filbert], lying in the palm of my hand, as it seemed to me, and it was as round as a ball. I looked at it with the eye of my understanding and thought: What can this be? I was amazed that it could last, for I thought that because of its littleness it would suddenly have fallen into nothing. And I was answered in my understanding: It lasts and always will, because God loves it; and thus everything has being through the love of God.
>
> In this little thing I saw three properties. The first is that God made it, the second is that God loves it, the third is that God preserves it. But what did I see in it? It is that God is the Creator and the protector and the lover.[30]

Holding this little hazelnut, say to yourself, "God made me. God loves me. God keeps me."

▌ Silence
(15–20 minutes)

▌ Rest and Journaling
(5–10 minutes)

Ask the participants to record in their journals any thoughts or images they had during the silence.

▌ Reflection Questions
(5–10 minutes)

Ask the participants to ponder the following questions and respond to them in their journal.

1. Was the hazelnut a vehicle for you to experience God, or a hindrance? Why or why not?
2. Did feelings surface about how God looks after you? Can you describe them here?

▌ Small Group Sharing
(10–15 minutes)

Ask the participants to share their responses in pairs or small groups.

▌ Plenary
(5–15 minutes)

Ask the participants to share an insight they learned from the small group sharing.

▌ Closing Prayer Circle
(5–10 minutes)

Ask the participants to gather in a circle for prayer. Refer to page 41 for suggestions.

▌ Homework

Note: For retreats, a follow-up activity is to have small groups pool ideas for other objects that might be used and to discuss how the use of something this ordinary can bring us closer to God.

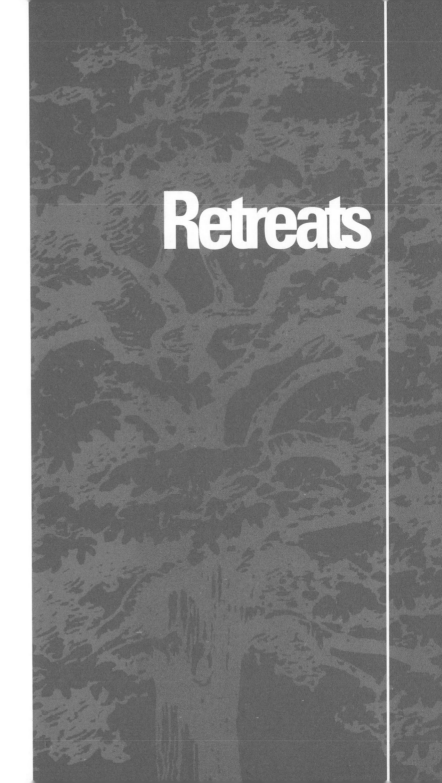

Retreats 8

▌ General Information

With the exception of the first retreat model, this chapter primarily contains a sample of resource materials and suggested activities for retreat themes, not a collection of finished products. It is hoped that these materials will motivate leaders to develop creative designs that nurture spiritual growth. Retreats are most successful if they are developed specifically with the participating group in mind and not presented as a performed "package." Variations in the time allotted, in the nature of the group, in the facility where the retreat is being held, as well as in available materials, affect the kind of planning needed.

▌ Schedules

It is helpful if, when planning a retreat, the time together is viewed in "blocks." This keeps people (both leader and participants) from becoming overly concerned with agendas. It leaves space for the unexpected—those grace-filled moments when something unplanned is welcomed and incorporated into the schedule. The basic "blocks" are fairly obvious: Morning—Afternoon—Evening. Within each, allow for a break (see sample schedule below).

Sample Weekend Retreat Schedule

Friday	Saturday	Sunday
Evening	*Morning*	*Morning*
Arrival after supper	Morning prayer*	Morning prayer
Introduction	Breakfast	Breakfast
Opening remarks	Block #2	Block #5
Block #1	(with break in middle)	Closing worship
Evening prayer (Vespers)	*Afternoon*	(with opportunity
Optional social time	Lunch	for sharing)
(snacks and beverages)	Block #3**	Communion, if desired
	Free time	Lunch/Departure
	Evening	
	Dinner	
	Block #4	
	Evening prayer	

*Many groups may not want to have morning prayer before breakfast, so scheduling it after breakfast may prevent a poor turnout. However, participants may be willing to try something new. In spirituality retreats, experiencing prayer together first thing in the morning has the effect of setting the tone for the day's events. It is obviously an aid to centering, as opposed to scattering—which happens when social agendas and personal needs get the priority of the day.

**The afternoons are usually designed in one of three ways: (1) free time first, (2) free time last, and (3) free time sandwiched between two shorter sessions. Depending on the leadership, the topic, the retreat facility, the expectations of the group, and the weather, a decision could be made favoring any of the three. However, be sure that the third option does not end up with two major presentations on either side of it. Trying to accomplish too much defeats the purpose of the retreat. It is not a "working" retreat. Above all else, the goal of the retreat is to help participants relax into God's presence. A pushed or rushed agenda will become all too apparent. I have been guilty of doing this, a few times at least, in my eagerness to offer everything possible. After all, I would reason, this may be my only chance! Stuff them; they rarely get such an opportunity for soul food! Unfortunately, I've learned that it only tends to produce spiritual indigestion instead of a good spiritual diet.

Free Time

Too often, even "free time" is planned. The group is kidnapped into someone's prearranged decision, or "what we've always done," or peer pressure. This is one of the "spaces" that should be honored most of all in spirituality events. Most people do not treat themselves to this "time apart," and free time provides for that. It is not subject to judgment. Choices might be given as suggestions for those who desire creative ways to spend their time with God. However, be sure that resting and taking a nap is included!

Content

Content is the part of the retreat that fills in those "blocks" referred to above. In the material that follows, you will find many ideas for addressing a theme. No time is given, since each is dependent on the size of the group and the way one implements the suggestion. In addition to the ideas given here, you will also want to refer to the prayer experience models in chapter 7. These ideas can be adapted in length, content, and process to reflect the particular objective desired—whether it be a particular Scripture passage, theme, or spiritual practice.

Use of Music

Music is basically an untapped resource in spirituality. When asked how people experience God, however, many will respond "through music." This may take the form of church music, classical music, or alternative music, to name only a few. Unfortunately, when planning spirituality events, leaders assume that they themselves must be musical, or have musically gifted participants, to use music in their sessions. With all the tapes and compact discs available today, there is little excuse for not including music in retreat programs. Some ideas are offered in this chapter, with additional resources listed in chapter 10.

Worship Experiences

Very often retreat worship is a mini-version of Sunday worship with a few variations added. It may not occur to people that worship need not look or feel the same. Retreats provide opportunities for fresh ways of experiencing God's presence. Allow the Spirit more freedom to be at work within the group by providing spaces for silence and reflection. A few "starters" for variations are as follows:

1. Instead of preprinted litanies, encourage participants to contribute an original prayer or poem, artwork, comments or insights, or Scripture passages.

2. Plan forms of worship that will motivate and encourage the participants to listen. Don't create an atmosphere that lends itself to jumping up and down for responses, or even following hymn words. Participants should just be present, focusing on listening. Any words spoken, such as in Scripture, prayers, or poetry, should be *very* brief and interspersed with silence. Remember that many words can get in the way of the Word.

3. Use music from tapes or compact discs to set a mood, to introduce Scripture, or to guide a meditation. Hymns can be played, calling people to listen to the words instead of finding and singing the notes.

4. Introduce a nonthreatening form of guided relaxation, such as the meditation exercises on page 24. Consider using one as a benediction or prior to the passing of the peace.

Retreat Theme

1

❚ Simple Gifts: Nurturing Our Desire for God*

---

*With special thanks to the members of the Vienna Presbyterian Church in Vienna, Virginia, who helped with the planning of this retreat.

Day One
(Friday evening)

❚ Introduction

Express appreciation for all the preparations. Ask the participants to take time to notice the posters you have displayed on the walls. Lead the group in "Prayer for a Busy Day" (page 144). *Read aloud the following or state in your own words.*

Why Are We Here?

- to nurture our spirit
- to spend time with God (we're called to do that)
- to relax, rest, and be refreshed (give self permission for that)
- not to rush around or be anything to anyone or to do anything
- to listen to the sound and the silence
- to experience some familiar things and some new things

The goal is not to get anything out of the day as much as it is to feel that we have been in the presence of God. So—be open to whatever may be God's gift to you today. No expectations, just an openness.

The theme of this retreat is "Simple Gifts." We will be open to what comes through to us as we use several different approaches. Be open. Remember God honors your heart's desire.

May you know the peace of Christ in our time together.

Directions

Review the following with the participants:

Folders
Use folders with two inside pockets for including materials from the retreat.

Journals
See "Explanations" on page 32.

Candle
See "Explanations" on page 32.

Place
Just as you remember to be at church for worship at a particular time, reserve a special time for being with God at home—no matter how brief.

You may have the same environment at home with whatever symbols you find appropriate. These symbols become associated with your expectation to be with God. It should be a quiet place, with no distractions like being near the phone, a stack of reading material, bills to pay, or grocery lists.

Expectations

None. Please don't look for any sound and light shows. Simply be willing to be present to whatever happens or doesn't happen. Your willingness to be open and present is more important than what you are feeling. Don't look for anything. Enjoy the moment of doing nothing.

❚ Opening Remarks

1. *Read aloud the following or state in your own words.*

Doing nothing. Ingrained in us is the notion that there's got to be something we can *do* to be more faithful and shore up our neglected souls. It doesn't occur to us to *do nothing*! Let us remember that prayer without silence and listening is only a one-way street.

2. Use the excerpts in chapter 5 (pages 15–17). Then tell the story of the hermit (page 13) and/or The Talkative Lover (page 17).

If things seem stiff and stilted at this point, have everyone stand, stretch, and prepare for the first session by taking a two-minute standing break.

❚ Example for Block #1— Prayers for Slowing Down

See Model A. Breath Prayer from Scripture (Psalm 62:1) on page 42. Consider using this presentation.

Silence
(approximately 15 minutes)

Journal Questions

Note: For those who are right-brained and prefer to express themselves nonverbally, place a table in the room with crayons, markers, paper, and so on.

Ask the participants to respond to the following questions in their journals.

1. How was the breath prayer for you? Was God present in and through your breath? How?

2. Did you notice any resistance or blocks? What were they?

Sharing

After the participants have finished writing or drawing, ask them to find a partner and share their experience using the following questions.

1. What was this experience like for you?

2. What other Scripture verses might you want to use as a breath prayer? Why?

Then gather the participants into one group and ask the following questions:

1. Is there anything you would like to share with the whole group?

2. Are there any verses you would like to offer for us to add? (If so, write these on newsprint. Give handout with starters that they can add to.)

3. Inform the group that they might also enjoy the same practice using a word, such as a name for God or Jesus.

❚ Evening Prayer (Vespers)

Sing and Dance

Learn a dance to the Shaker hymn, "A Gift to Be Simple," and have a member of the group prepared to teach this using the motions for the dance found on page 91.

Enjoy this time together. It *is* worship, though different in form for most people.

Scripture Reading

Choose one of the following:

1. Ask for three volunteers to read 1 Kings 19:1–12. The script of this passage can be found on page 92.

2. Read the meditation "Silence" based on 1 Kings 19:1–18 on page 93. Ask participants to reflect silently on the words.

Prayer

Ask for a volunteer to read aloud *A Cry for Mercy* on page 94.

Meditation

Read aloud the following:

I Simply Come To Be With You

God of earthquake, wind, and fire,
   and of the still small voice,
   and of the silence of the silence,
I bring my presence
   to your presence
   as a gift to you—
The only gift that I in fact can
      give—
For all the other gifts
   are gifts that you have given
   which I can but return to you.

I do not come to speak or hear.
I do not come to think or do,
But Lord of Lords, and very God,
I simply come to be with you.

(Anne Shotwell)[1]

Hymn

Sing "Dear Lord and Father of Mankind" or "Spirit of God, Descend Upon My Heart."

Day Two
(Morning Prayer)

Prelude

Have music playing as people arrive. Suggestions are the extended version of "Jesu, Joy of Man's Desiring" by Kobialka[2]; "Morning Has Broken" as arranged for harmonica and harp.[3]

Hymn

Sing "Morning Has Broken."

Movement

Have some guided relaxation (body prayer; see pages 25–26); guide the participants through some stretching and moving.

Scripture Reading

Psalm 42:1–5 (*The Psalms: A New Translation for Prayer and Worship*)[4]

Prayer

Distribute copies of "God Be in My Head" on page 95. Guide group in becoming aware of each part of their body as the prayer is repeated *very slowly*. Read in unison or sing. Repeat the prayer together slowly.

Guided Relaxation

Ask the participants to stand. Do the meditation exercises on page 24. Emphasize being receptive to God's love and gifts.

Closing

Close with singing and moving to "A Gift to Be Simple" (page 91).

▌ Example for Block #2— Using Scripture for Prayer

Use the directions from Model B. Praying with Scripture (Psalm 139) found on page 44.

Tell the participants that they will be using one of three passages of Scripture. All passages will be read by the retreat leader and then the participants will be asked to select one to use in a small group. These are passages that will enable the participants to put themselves "in the picture." After the participants have made their selections, ask them to proceed to small groups where the designated leader will give directions.

Give previously selected small group leaders their instructions (see "Directions for Small Group Leaders," page 96) and distribute to each person copies of the stories on pages 97–99.

The Wedding Banquet
Bar-timaeus/Bat-timaeus
The Rich Man

You may also want to consider playing "The Wedding Banquet" (see page 100). This song from the seventies—now enjoying a revival—has a lilting tune and words that lend a contemporary touch as well as some humor. To order, please write to Medical Mission Sisters, 77 Sherman Street, Hartford, CT 06105 and request *Songlines: Hymns, Songs, Rounds, and Refrains for Prayer and Praise* (paperback) or "Joy Is Like the Rain" (audiocassette).

▌ Example for Block #3— Praying the Psalms

Two plans are included here. Read through both and select the one that you feel would work best with the group.

Plan One: Writing Your Own Psalm

1. Give directions from "Writing Your Own Psalm" (see page 34).

2. Tell the group that when they are finished, they are to take their journals into the sanctuary (or chapel or a designated room) and pick up a handout on their way in.

3. Explain that they will be picking up "Page A" (page 101) and then will be given "Page B" (page 102) later. Ask them to follow the directions as written.

4. Play the tape of Psalm 23 (Grail Version), from *The Gelineau Psalms*, while the participants follow directions on "Page B."

Plan Two:
Using *Lectio Divina*

Another form of praying with Scripture has its origins in the Middle Ages. See Model B. Praying with Scripture (Psalm 139) on page 44 for a simple version. Distribute "Prayer Before Reading," *Lectio Divina* directions, and the two psalms (pages 105–106). They could also be used as take-home pages to stimulate a contemplative practice.

Other sources of Scripture passages for meditation can be found in the following:

- The lectionary used in worship
- *A Guide to Prayer for All God's People,* by Reuben Job and Norman Shawchuck. Lists the Scriptures for each week (from the lectionary), including each day, as well as a collection of writings and prayers.
- Other psalms, using a variety of versions
- *Too Deep for Words: Rediscovering* Lectio Divina (with 500 Scripture Texts for Prayer), by Thelma Hall.

John of the Cross used an adaptation of Luke 11:9 to express another view of this form:

> Seek in *reading,*
> and you will find in *meditation;*
> knock in *prayer*
> and it will be opened to you in *contemplation.*

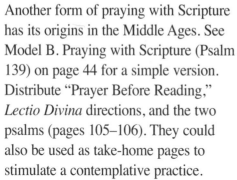

❚ Example for Block #4— Seeing God in the Ordinary

Use Model M. Seeing God in the Ordinary on pages 80–81. You will need to provide each participant with a hazelnut (filbert).

❚ Closing Worship and Communion

Have the group put together the elements of worship that have been meaningful for them for closing worship. Let them also be responsible for doing these things.

Hymn
"Morning Has Broken" (from Morning Prayer, page 88)

Scripture
Isaiah 55:1–2, 10–11

Song
"The Wedding Banquet" (see page 100)

Scripture
Romans 8:26–39

Prayer
By a member of the group

Song and Dance:
"A Gift to Be Simple" (page 91). Share how we have experienced God's presence or our desire for God during our time together.

Communion

Closing Song
"God, Guide Us Home" (see Model L. Sound and Silence, page 78.)

Benediction
Said to each other by name, as we "passed the peace": "[*name*] may you know the sheer silence of God."[5]

A Gift to Be Simple*

Opening formation: a circle, all facing center.

'Tis the gift to be simple, 'tis the gift to be free:
All take four steps toward the center, beginning with the right foot (r, l, r, l). Hands are held in front of the body; about waist height, palms facing upward. Initiated by a gentle wrist movement, the hands pulse upward and downward. (This up-and-down movement with upturned hands was thought of as a gesture to receive grace.)

'Tis the gift to come down where we ought to be:
All take four steps back to place (r, l, r, l). The palms face downward as you walk backward, and shake in a small down-and-up direction. This movement, with turned down palms, was used to signify shaking out bad influences, or "all that is carnal." (There is a Shaker song with the words, "Come life, Shaker life, come life eternal, shake, shake out of me all that is carnal.")

And when we find ourselves in the place just right, we will be in the valley of love and delight: Repeat the above pattern; four steps into the center and four steps back to place.

When true simplicity is gained: Bring hands to prayer position (palms together, fingertips pointing upward). Step to the right with the right foot and bring the left foot to meet the right, bending both knees. Reverse to the left on the words, "simplicity is gained."

To bow and to bend we shall not be ashamed: Repeat the above pattern (stepping and bending to the right and then to the left).

To turn, turn will be our delight: Keeping hands in the same prayer position, turn in place by making a small circle to the right (step r, l, r, l). End facing the center.

Till by turning, turning we come round right:
(Make a small circle to the left, stepping l, r, l, r.)

*From *The Spirit Moves*, by Carla Desola. Copyright © 1977 The Liturgical Conference, 8750 Georgia Avenue, Suite 123, Silver Spring, MD 20910-3621. All rights reserved. Used with permission.

Scripture Reading:
1 Kings 19:1–12

Characters:
Narrator (plain script)
Angel of the Lord (*italics*)
Elijah (**bold script**)

Narrator: Ahab told Jezebel all that Elijah had done, and how he had killed all the prophets with the sword. Then Jezebel sent a messenger to Elijah, saying, "So may the gods do to me, and more also, if I do not make your life like the life of one of them by this time tomorrow."

Then he was afraid; he got up and fled for his life, and came to Beersheba, which belongs to Judah; he left his servant there. But he himself went a day's journey into the wilderness, and came and sat down under a solitary broom tree. He asked that he might die.

Elijah: "It is enough; now, O LORD, take away my life, for I am no better than my ancestors."

Narrator: Then he lay down under the broom tree and fell asleep. Suddenly an angel touched him and said to him,

Angel of the Lord: *"Get up and eat."*

Narrator: He looked, and there at his head was a cake baked on hot stones, and a jar of water. He ate and drank, and lay down again. The angel of the LORD came a second time, touched him, and said,

Angel of the Lord: *"Get up and eat, otherwise the journey will be too much for you."*

Narrator: He got up, and ate and drank; then he went in the strength of that food forty days and forty nights to Horeb the mount of God. At that place he came to a cave, and spent the night there. Then the word of the LORD came to him, saying,

Angel of the Lord: *"What are you doing here, Elijah?"*

Elijah: "I have been very zealous for the LORD, the God of hosts; for the Israelites have forsaken your covenant, thrown down your altars, and killed your prophets with the sword. I alone am left, and they are seeking my life, to take it away."

Angel of the Lord: *"Go out and stand on the mountain before the LORD, for the LORD is about to pass by."*

Narrator: Now there was a great wind, so strong that it was splitting mountains and breaking rocks in pieces before the LORD, but the LORD was not in the wind; and after the wind an earthquake, but the LORD was not in the earthquake; and after the earthquake a fire, but the LORD was not in the fire; and after the fire a sound of sheer silence.

Silence*

> I ask no dream, no prophet ecstasies,
> no sudden rending of the veil of clay,
> no angel visitant, no op'ning skies;
> but take the dimness of my soul away.

A companion on the path to hope today is Elijah, who seems to be a strange choice from almost three thousand years ago. He is helpful for his very strangeness. His king called him the "troubler," and his queen was out to kill him. The situation of the prophet was hopeless, so he prayed that he might die. Tired from fleeing, Elijah slept under a broom tree. "Suddenly an angel touched him and said to him, 'Get up and eat.' " Awakened, he was given food there and strength for journeying to the mount of God.

Atop it, he experienced a rock-splitting wind, followed by an earthquake, fire, and then "a sound of sheer silence" in which the Lord spoke to him and gave him a mission, plus the power he needed for it, and then reasons for hope.

Strange and different from our experience, but still helpful, are Elijah and his story. Without any dreams, any ecstasies, opening skies, or angel visitants, we who seek meaning for our missions, the power required for them, and reasons for hope profit on occasion from the "sound of sheer silence." A hinting, barely whispering divine word reveals what we need and crave.

Not fireworks and earthquakes but the sound of sheer silence, now, as then, eliminates the dimness of soul and makes the path bright.

*Reprinted by permission from *Our Hope for Years To Come*, by Martin Marty, p. 24.
Copyright © 1995 Augsburg Fortress.

A Cry for Mercy*

Why, O Lord, is it so hard for me to keep my heart directed toward you? Why do the many little things I want to do, and the many people I know, keep crowding my mind, even during the hours that I am totally free to be with you and you alone? Why does my mind wander off in so many directions, and why does my heart desire the things that lead me astray? Are you not enough for me? Do I keep doubting your love and care, your mercy and grace? Do I keep wondering, in the center of my being, whether you will give me all I need if I just keep my eyes on you?

Please accept my distractions, my fatigue, my irritations, and my faithless wanderings. You know me more deeply and fully than I know myself. You love me with a greater love than I can love myself. You even offer me more than I can desire. Look at me, see me in all my misery and inner confusion, and let me sense your presence in the midst of my turmoil. All I can do is show myself to you. Yet, I am afraid to do so. I am afraid that you will reject me. But I know—with the knowledge of faith—that you desire to give me your love. The only thing you ask of me is not to hide from you, not to run away in despair, not to act as if you were a relentless despot.

Take my tired body, my confused mind, and my restless soul into your arms and give me rest, simple quiet rest. Do I ask too much too soon? I should not worry about that. You will let me know. Come, Lord Jesus, come. Amen.

*From *A Cry for Mercy: Prayers from the Genesee*, by Henri J. M. Nouwen, pp. 26–27. Copyright © 1981 by Henri J. M. Nouwen. Used by permission of Doubleday, a division of Bantam Doubleday Dell Publishing Group, Inc.

God Be in My Head*

"Sarum Primer," 1558   H. Walford Davies, 1869–1941

*"God Be in My Head," *The Pilgrim Hymnal* (New York: Pilgrim Press, 1985), no. 543.

Directions for Small Group Leaders

1 Tell the group that you are going to read the passage aloud twice and that there will be fifteen minutes of silence afterward to "be with" that passage. They are to do nothing during the silence except let the words sift through their hearts (not minds as in a Bible study)!

2 After fifteen minutes of silence, quietly draw the group back by tapping a glass or using a bell.

3 Give out copies of the passage to each person.

4 Ask them to respond in their journals to those questions. If some wish to draw instead of write, they may feel free to do so.

5 After about ten or fifteen minutes (or whatever seems right), call the group together for any sharing that they would like to do relating to this experience. This sharing can be free-form or guided, as you sense the group you are facilitating.

6 Please honor the break time and see that people are not kept during that period.

The Wedding Banquet

One of the dinner guests, on hearing this, said to him, "Blessed is the one who will eat bread in the kingdom of God!" Then Jesus said to him, "Someone gave a great dinner and invited many. At the time for the dinner he sent his slave to say to those who had been invited, 'Come; for everything is ready now.' But they all alike began to make excuses. The first said to him, 'I have bought a piece of land, and I must go out and see it; please accept my regrets.' Another said, 'I have bought five yoke of oxen, and I am going to try them out; please accept my regrets.' Another said, 'I have just been married, and therefore I cannot come.' So the slave returned and reported this to his master. Then the owner of the house became angry and said to his slave, 'Go out at once into the streets and lanes of the town and bring in the poor, the crippled, the blind, and the lame.' And the slave said, 'Sir, what you ordered has been done, and there is still room.' Then the master said to the slave, 'Go out into the road and lanes, and compel people to come in, so that my house may be filled. For I tell you, none of those who were invited will taste my dinner.'"

(Luke 14:15–24, NRSV)

Journal Questions

1. Was God/Jesus present for you in the silence? How?
2. Did you experience any difficulties, that is, resistance to "being with" the passage? Describe them.
3. Which person did you identify with in the story? Why?
4. If you were one of those who sent regrets, what kept you from the banquet?
5. How did this passage make you feel?
6. Write a short prayer expressing those feelings, whatever they were, to God.

Bar-timaeus
(Son of Timaeus)
Bat-timaeus
(Daughter of Timaeus)

They came to Jericho. As he and his disciples and a large crowd were leaving Jericho, [Battimaeus daughter] of Timaeus, a blind beggar, was sitting by the roadside. When she heard that it was Jesus of Nazareth, she began to shout out and say, "Jesus, Son of David, have mercy on me!" Many sternly ordered her to be quiet, but she cried out even more loudly, "Son of David, have mercy on me!" Jesus stood still and said, "Call her here." And they called the blind woman, saying to her, "Take heart; get up, he is calling you." So throwing off her cloak, she sprang up and came to Jesus. Then Jesus said to her, "What do you want me to do for you?" The blind woman said to him, "My teacher, let me see again." Jesus said to her, "Go; your faith has made you well." Immediately she regained her sight and followed him on the way.

(Mark 10:46–52, NRSV)

Journal Questions

1. Was God/Jesus present for you in the silence? How?
2. Did you experience any difficulties, that is, resistance to "being with" the passage?
3. How did you answer Jesus when he said, "What do you want me to do for you?"
4. Was this your heart's desire?
5. How did Jesus respond?
6. How did you feel?
7. Write a short prayer expressing those feelings to God.

The Rich Man

As he was setting out on a journey, a man ran up and knelt before him, and asked him, "Good Teacher, what must I do to inherit eternal life?" Jesus said to him, "Why do you call me good? No one is good but God alone. You know the commandments: 'You shall not murder; You shall not commit adultery; You shall not steal; You shall not bear false witness; You shall not defraud; Honor your father and mother.'"

He said to him, "Teacher, I have kept all these since my youth." Jesus, looking at him, loved him and said, "You lack one thing; go, sell what you own, and give the money to the poor, and you will have treasure in heaven; then come, follow me." When he heard this, he was shocked and went away grieving, for he had many possessions.

(Mark 10:17–22, NRSV)

Journal Questions

1. Was God/Jesus present for you in the silence? How?
2. Did you experience any difficulties, that is, resistance to "being with" the passage?
3. In what way did you identify with the man in the story?
4. What did *you* hear when Jesus said to you: "You lack one thing . . ."?
5. What would that mean for you?
6. Were you given any clues to possible stumbling blocks?
7. How did you feel?
8. Write a short prayer expressing those feelings, whatever they were, to God.

The Wedding Banquet*

Chorus:
I cannot come.
I cannot come to the banquet, don't trouble me now.
I have married a wife. I have bought me a cow.
I have fields and commitments that cost a pretty sum.
Pray, hold me excused, I cannot come.

A certain man held a feast on his fine estate in town.
He laid a festive table and wore a wedding gown.
He sent invitations to his neighbors far and wide
but when the meal was ready, each of them replied:
(Chorus)

The master rose up in anger, called his servants by
    name,
said, "Go into town, fetch the blind and the lame,
fetch the peasant and the pauper for this I have
    willed,
my banquet must be crowded, and my table must be
    filled." (Chorus)

When all the poor had assembled, there was still
    room to spare,
so the master demanded: "Go search everywhere,
to the highways and the byways and force them to
    come in.
My table must be filled before the banquet can
    begin." (Chorus)

Now God has written a lesson for the rest of
    humankind;
If we're slow in responding, He may leave us behind.
He's preparing a banquet for that great and glorious
    day.
When the Lord and Master calls us, be certain not
    to say: (Chorus)

*"The Wedding Banquet," words by Miriam Therese Winter.
Copyright © 1965 The Medical Mission Sisters.

Page A

Find a place *alone* in the sanctuary.

Read what you have written in your journal at least once.

This is your psalm. It is your way of crying out to God. Maybe you have unloaded your anger or sorrow or joy. Whatever, remember that even if what you have written is unacceptable to you, it is acceptable to God.

Now close your eyes and see yourself handing it to Jesus. Be with the scene for about ten minutes. You will hear a little bell calling you back. Take a moment to rest with that experience.

Until you hear the bell again, write anything down that you would like to remember.

Someone will pass out Page B after a few minutes.

When you hear the bell a third time, follow the directions on Page B.

Page B

Using Psalm 23

Listen to the music.

Let your ear and eye rest with the word or phrase that touches you most deeply.

Perhaps a line will match your psalm or be a response to your need.

Perhaps a word will offer comfort or healing, gratitude or courage.

Take that word or phrase into the silence that follows and breathe it in.

Be in silence until you hear the meditation bell.

Please leave the sanctuary quietly.

Psalm 23 (Grail Version)*
(Music by Joseph Gelineau)

The Lord is my shepherd; there is nothing I shall want.
Fresh and green are the pastures where he gives me repose.
Near restful waters he leads me, to revive my drooping spirit.

Antiphon:
The Lord is my shepherd;
Nothing shall I want.
He leads me by safe paths;
Nothing shall I fear.

He guides me along the right path; he is true to his name.
If I should walk in the valley of darkness no evil would I fear.
You are there with your crook and your staff; with these you give me
    comfort. (Antiphon)

You have prepared a banquet for me in the sight of my foes.
My head you have anointed with oil; my cup is overflowing. (Antiphon)

Surely goodness and kindness shall follow me all the days of my life.
In the Lord's own house shall I dwell, for ever and ever. (Antiphon)

Doxology:
To the Father and the Son give glory,
Give glory to the Spirit,
To God who is, who was, who will be
Forever and ever.

*From *The Psalms: An Inclusive Language Version Based on the Grail Translation from the Hebrew.* Copyright © 1963, 1986 Ladies of the Grail (England). Used by permission of G.I.A. Publications, Inc., Chicago, Illinois, exclusive agent. All rights reserved. This psalm can be heard on *The Gelineau Psalms,* translated and arranged by Joseph Gelineau. To order, write G.I.A. Publications, Inc., 7404 S. Mason Ave., Chicago, IL 60638.

Prayer Before Reading*

All-Seeing One,
above me, around me, within me.
Be my seeing as I read these sacred words.
Look down upon me
Look out from within me
Look all around me
See through my eyes
Hear through my ears
Feel through my heart
Touch me where I need to be touched;
    and when my heart is touched,
      give me the grace to lay down this Holy Book
      and ask significant questions:
Why has my heart been touched?
How am I to be changed through this touch?
All-Seeing One,
I need to change
I need to look a little more like You
May these sacred words change and transform me.

*From *A Tree Full of Angels*, by Macrina Wiederkehr. Copyright © 1988 by
  Macrina Wiederkehr. Reprinted by permission of HarperCollins Publishers, Inc.

Lectio Divina
(Divine Reading)*

Reading

Read the psalm, as you would put food in your mouth.

Meditation

"Chew" on it. Dig for a treasure in the passage. When something touches your heart, stop reading. God has given you a word to be a guest in your heart. Welcome it. Walk with it. Wrestle with it. Ask it questions. Allow it to nourish you. Receive its blessing. If nothing touches you, be still. God also speaks in silence and darkness.

Prayer

Pray your feelings. Maybe you can only stand in awe, rejoicing. That is prayer. Perhaps you weep. Or sing. Or tenderly talk to God. Or scream in anger. Or kneel with outstretched arms. Prayer is a link, a mutual yearning—straining—aching. Prayer is tasting life.

Contemplation

Having tasted, you respond. With complete abandon let yourself fall into the hands of the living God. Trust. Melt into God. Stop struggling. Surrender. Nothing is left except being in God.

Journaling

Write down the phrase that you used and any thoughts that you wish to record. Carry the phrase with you through the day.

Psalm 13 (Grail)*

How long, O Lord, will you forget me?
How long will you hide your face?
How long must I bear grief in my soul,
this sorrow in my heart day and night?
How long shall my enemy prevail?

Look at me, answer me, Lord my God!
Give light to my eyes lest I fall asleep
    in death,
lest my enemy say: "I have prevailed";
lest my foes rejoice to see my fall.

As for me, I trust in your merciful love.
Let my heart rejoice in your saving
    help.
Let me sing to the Lord for his
    goodness to me,
singing psalms to the name of the Lord,
    the Most High.

Psalm 40*

Oh, how I longed for the Lord,
    And God bent down, and heard my cry,
And brought me up from a desolate pit,
    Out of the muddy clay,
And set my feet on a rock,
    Making my steps firm and sure,
And put in my mouth a new song,
    A song of praise for our God.
Many people will see, and be awed,
    And will put their trust in the Lord.
Blessed are those who do so—
    Who put their trust in the Lord—
And do not turn to false gods
    That deceive them and lead them astray.
You have done great things;
    Lord God, you have worked such wonders.
And your intentions for us—
    No one can compare to you!
I could go on talking and talking;
    Your deeds are too many to tell.
You want no sacrificial gifts—
    You carved out my ears, I hear you;
You seek no offerings for sin or praise,
    So I said, "I will simply bring myself."
I desire to do what pleases my God,
    To have your teaching deep within me.
I bring good news to the whole congregation;
    Lord, you know that I am not silent!

I don't hide your justice within my own mind;
    I speak of your true power to save us.
I do not conceal your loyal love
    Or your truth from the great congregation.
Lord, don't withhold your compassion from me;
    May your faithful love always protect me.
For wrongs past counting surround me;
    My sins overtake me and blind me.
They outnumber the hairs on my head,
    And all my courage has left me.
O Lord, be willing to save me;
    Hurry, O Lord, to help me.
Completely shame and humiliate those
    Who seek to take my life.
Let them turn back in disgrace
    For wanting to hurt me.
Let them shudder with shame
    Who laughed aloud at me.
But let all those who seek you
    Be joyful and happy in you.
Let those who love your salvation declare:
    "The Lord is eternally great!"
But I am wretched and poor;
    Consider me, O Lord!
It is you who rescue and aid me;
    My God, do not delay!

*From *The Psalms: A New Translation for Prayer and Worship,* translated by Gary Chamberlain, pp. 64–66. Copyright © 1984 by The Upper Room. Used by permission of Upper Room Books.

Retreat Theme

2

▌ Images of God

▌ Suggested Activities

1. Colors That Represent God

Ask the participants to use crayons to produce a picture of colors that represents God for them. When everyone has finished, ask each to write in pencil on the back what was being conveyed. Share in groups of four by asking: What do others see? What does it say about God?

2. When I Was a Child . . .

Ask the participants to go back in their lives and try to remember how they pictured God when they were five to eight years old. Ask: What was God to you? How did you see God as a child? Then, in their journals, ask them to complete one of the following sentences:

- To me God was . . .
- God seemed like . . .
- I felt that God . . .

When everyone has finished, share in groups of four. Write all ideas, concepts, images, and feelings on newsprint, then go back and put a + (plus) or – (minus) beside *present* views on these.

3. How Different People Picture God

Explain the difference between transcendence (being beyond the world) and immanence (being in the world). Then give input from some of the excerpts appearing on pages 108–109, or from other sources you might have. The following sources may also be helpful:

- Ann Ulanov's *Picturing God* (see especially the last chapter)[6]
- Virginia R. Mollenkott's *The Divine Feminine: The Biblical Imagery of God as Female*[7] (see especially the following chapters: Some Lessons from History, pp. 8–9; God as Mother Eagle, pp. 83–89; The Divine Milieu, pp. 106–109; Some Suggestions and Conclusions, pp. 110–113)
- Thomas R. Hawkins' *The Potter and the Clay: Meditations on Spiritual Growth*[8]
- Fynn's *Mister God, This is Anna*,[9] especially pp. 38–40, 155–156, 169–171 (Maybe the participants could be asked to write their own "Dear Mr. God")
- Alice Walker's *The Color Purple*,[10] especially pages 176–179

With That 90 Percent Rating, Is God Pressing Too Hard?*

If God was only someone else . . . . But, no, he (she?) insists on being God. God puts, or tries to put, himself (herself?) in charge of everything. I mean everything—including our very lives.

I have read that approximately 90 percent of all Americans believe in God. God must be flattered. Have any of our presidents achieved a 90 percent rating? Or anyone for anything? It may be true that a lot of people said yes because they weren't taking the matter very seriously. Even so, the polling reveals that there were only a few hard noses who emphatically said no.

Now for the big question: What is the nature of this God who is so well liked? A Sunday school teacher once described God as a grand old man with a soft white beard, looking down on his children through a Santa Claus face. A kind of non-questioning guy who would be glad to lend you a few bucks 'til payday.

A country singer referred to God as her "buddy." Buddies can be very close. I can only think God is very pleased to be a part of her entourage. I gladly pay $17.50 just to be one of 5,000 to hear her sing.

A fighter years ago referred to God as "the Man upstairs." That nickname has stuck around for decades and reveals another aspect of how we look on God. We want God to be near, particularly when things are going wrong, but the rest of the time God can stay in his room upstairs. I think you get the drift. There are times when God is a drag. God is no Spuds MacKenzie, so when God tags along we feel compelled to travel in the slow lane.

And this brings me to what I think could be God's big mistake—God's insistence on being God. God is pushing his (her?) luck. Someday God could wake up to discover that he (she?) has dropped 20 points in the popularity polls. Right now God is riding the crest of the wave. God had better leave well enough alone.

What God doesn't understand, apparently, is that he (she?) is not central to our lives. God is just one of the options. Like reading M. Scott Peck, collecting postcards, taking a course in the arts, or beginning a regimen of aerobics exercising. God is someone we might "get into," given the appropriate circumstances.

There are many things we do without God. I sometimes wonder if God knows that. Days go by, even years go by, without our ever needing to contact him (her?). And if we ever do need to get in touch, God should be easy to reach. There are Bibles everywhere. Besides, within every church there is a handful of women who have been praying to God for years. In an emergency they could likely "patch us through" in a hurry. They may rank up there with mobile phones.

Unfortunately, I don't think God will ever consider changing. God is determined to be God.

The changing is to come at our end. The situation is alarming. God has recently taken to looking us in the eye and using words like *faithfulness* and *obedience*. How can we be all that we can be with God leaning on us? I'm even beginning to feel guilty about my misty eyes when I hear Frank Sinatra singing, "I did it my way."

I brought this ugly matter to the attention of our pastor. "I liked God better when he could be manipulated," I whined. "You know, when he was into being all-loving, all-forgiving, and all-understanding.

"All I ever wanted was to have everything go my way. It wouldn't be so bad, either. I mean, you'd see one sweet guy. Of course if you ever crossed me . . . I mean, someone has to be in charge, right?"

*From Levi Tickus, "With That 90 Percent Rating, Is God Pressing Too Hard?" *Presbyterian Survey*, January/February 1989, p. 82. Used by permission. This is a satirical article related to God images.

*The images of God are many, he said, calling them "the masks of eternity" that both cover and reveal "The Face of Glory." . . . God assumes such different masks in different cultures, yet how it is that comparable stories can be found in these divergent traditions—stories of creation, of virgin births, incarnations, death and resurrection, second comings, and judgment days. He liked the insight of the Hindu scripture: "Truth is one; the sages call it by many names." All our names and images for God are masks, he said, signifying the ultimate reality that by definition transcends language and art. A myth is a mask of God, too—a metaphor for what lies behind the visible world. However, the mystic traditions differ, he said; they are in accord in calling us to a deeper awareness of the very act of living itself. The unpardonable sin, in Campbell's book, was the sin of inadvertence, of not being alert, not quite awake.

*From the "Introduction," in *The Power of Myth*, by Joseph Campbell and Bill Moyers, p. xvii. Copyright © 1988 by Apostrophe S Productions, Inc., and Bill Moyers and Alfred Van der Marck Editions, Inc., for itself and the estate of Joseph Campbell. Used by permission of Doubleday, a division of Bantam Doubleday Dell Publishing Group, Inc.

Unreal Gods*

1. Resident policeman (conscience)
2. Parental hangover (gospel of guilt; carryover of our father)
3. Grand old man (Sunday school children—grandfather image; "old" person)
4. Meek-and-mild (soft and sentimental childish conception; sweet tenderness)
5. Absolute perfection ("100%" standard . . . terrible tyrant; can never measure up; fantasy—produces paralysis; perfection not perfectionist)
6. Heavenly bosom (psychological escapism; God says, "Come unto me" but also "Go out in my name")
7. God-in-a-box (no one has a corner on God)
8. Managing director—of vast universe (not interested in me; model God on basis of knowledge of self)
9. Second-hand God (through others' words, fiction, religion misrepresentation)
10. Perennial grievance (pity me; prayer unanswered)
11. Pale Galilean (no joy)
12. Projected image (a prop to our self-esteem)

   True ideal stimulates, encourages, and produces likeness to itself.

*Adapted from *Your God Is Too Small*, by J. B. Phillips (New York: Macmillan, 1961.)

4. How Differently We See God in Nature

Use slides, either your own or purchased ones. Each person selects one slide that best illustrates for him or her a way that helps them "see" God. They also write a one-sentence statement about the slide, such as, "For the deserts and dry lands from which we learn patience and trust. . . ." Then these are shown in the closing worship as a form of sharing. Response could then be, "Thank you, God, for being with us."

5. How Differently We Experience God in God's House

Ask the participants to gather in the sanctuary in total silence, waiting, noticing, listening. Ask them to notice any symbols, feelings, smells, textures, colors, or sounds. When the bell rings, have the participants write in their journals about those things that spoke to them of God and those which might have been distractions, emphasizing that this is okay, too.

6. How Different Artists Depict God

Use reproductions of art that depict God (e.g., Michelangelo's face of God as creator; Rodin's Hand of God). Ask the participants to ponder the following:

- What do these say to us today? to you personally?
- How have the arts contributed to our ways of "seeing" God?
- Consider music (e.g., *The Messiah*), art, and literature (Gerard Manley Hopkins, *The Grandeur of God*) in addition to contemporary material.

7. How Differently We See God's Characteristics

Use Bible study. Distribute the handout on page 113 and ask the participants to follow the instructions.

8. Windows to God

Have a group of objects assembled on a table. (Could be center of worship later.) Ask the participants to observe them and note the particular ones that distinctly draw them to associate that object with the holy. Ask them to name these objects in their journals and write a brief paragraph for each about why it claimed their attention. Tell the participants that they may handle them (if they'd like) and, during the silence, to let God speak to them through these objects. Objects, symbols, and icons, may be used—anything that can be seen as a window to God; anything that is ordinary *or* set apart can be used here.

9. Who Is the God I Pray To?

See Ulanov's "Picturing God."[11] Ask the participants to describe the "I am" for them in prayer. Ask, Is there an image, a feeling, a presence, a quality, or nothing—space?

10. Music That Helps Us to Focus on God

Gather in the sanctuary and ask the participants to find a place that is all their own. Ask them to prepare to listen to the various sounds they will hear. Specifics about the pieces played are given only at the end of the session and are not listed or named at the time played in order to give less attention to the intellectual temptation to grasp and label.

After they hear each selection, ask them to take a moment to write in their journals how the music relaxed them and helped them to focus. Ask them to note any images or memories that seemed to guide them toward God and assisted them in being in God's presence. The following are some suggestions for music:

- "Stay Here and Watch with Me" (Taizé chant)
- "Morning"—Grieg (Galway, flute)
- "Let Us Break Bread Together"—Jessye Norman (solo)
- "Eternal Spring and Silver Moon" (from *Silk Road* by Kitaro, synthesizer)
- "Slavic Liturgy" (men's chorus)
- "The Lost Chord" (organ and Mormon Tabernacle Choir)
- "Immortal, Invisible"—The Huddersfield Choral Society
- Tibetan Bells/Inner Vistas
- Finale from *Les Misérables* ("To Love Another Person Is to See the Face of God")
- A selection from Handel's *Messiah*

11. Poetry That Helps Us to Consider God

Distribute copies of excerpts of the poems on page 114. Ask the participants to read them (or to follow along as they are read aloud) and consider how they relate to each other? Ask them to ponder the following question and respond in their journals: How does your becoming the image of God affect your "picture" of God?

12. The Journey Is Home

Show the video *The Journey Is Home*.[12] This provocative video can be used with a variety of groups. It can be liberating to some and offensive to others, but it plants seeds for thought. People should be encouraged to jot down any notes about what they want to remember while seeing the video. Hopefully, it will stir viewers to reflect on their own faith journey.

Read aloud the following to the group or state in your own words.

This is the story of a woman, then 80 or 82, and her faith journey. She was a pioneer in many fields, among which were civil rights in the 1930s, and seeing God in more than patriarchal images. She speaks in a homey way that appeals to all ages. She was raised in Appalachia and returned to do model studies with children after being influenced by Jean Piaget, the Swiss psychologist who studied children's thought processes. She later taught at Drew Divinity School from where she retired.

After viewing *The Journey Is Home*, ask the participants to respond in their journals to the following questions:

- What did you hear?
- In what ways did this video speak to you?
- In your faith journey, have any images been shattered? (Nelle claims to have had certain images shattered in her own life.)
- Did the story evoke any emotional reactions? If so, what kind?

13. Our Usual "Picturing" of God

Have large posters displayed around the room with the following words or pictures: grandfather, Santa, crown, dove, fire, rainbow, judge, potter, and so forth.

Ask the participants to stand by the poster that most closely resembles their usual picture of God. Then, have one person from each area explain why that word or picture on the poster most resembles his or her "picture" of God. Then as a total group, discuss the following:

- What attributes come from these images?
- What practices have we adopted in everyday life that reinforce the positive and/or negative aspects of these images?

14. Suggestions for Worship

Thomas Emswiler and Sharon Neufer Emswiler, in *Wholeness in Worship,* offer these words:

God's image is not limited to one place, one time, one religion, or one person. Rather it pervades the universe from the tiniest atom to the highest mountain. God is all and yet beyond all that we know. As Christians we affirm that this all embracing power is love. . . . Scholars tell us that the word *God* is probably derived from the original Indo-Germanic word *ghu-to*, "the called one" or "the one who is called." We are here because in some way or other we have felt the call of this one we have named God.[13]

15. Suggestions for Hymns

- "God, You Spin the Whirling Planets" (Jane Parker Huber)
- "On Wings of Morning" (Jane Parker Huber)
- "God Be in My Head"
- "Holy, Holy, Holy"
- "How Great Thou Art"
- "O God, We Bear the Imprint of Your Face" (Shirley Erena Murray)

16. Suggestions for Prayers

God be in my head,
And in my understanding;
God be in my eyes,
And in my looking;
God be in my mouth,
And in my speaking;
God be in my heart,
And in my thinking;
God be at mine end,
And at my departing.
                    (Sarum Primer)[14]

O Lord, how helpless I am
        when I try to talk to You about
                yourself!
How can I call You anything but the
        God of my life?
And what have I said with that title,
        when no name is really
                adequate?
I'm constantly tempted to creep
        away from You
    in utter discouragement,
    back to the things that are more
        comprehensible,
    to things with which my heart
            feels so much more at
        home
    than it does with Your
        mysteriousness.
                    (Karl Rahner)[15]

17. Suggestion for a Grace

For all your goodness Lord, we
        give you thanks.
Thanks for the food we eat, and for
        the friends we meet.
For each new day we greet, we give
        you thanks.
            (To the tune of "Die Musici,"
            usually found in camp or
            international songbooks)

18. Suggestions for Scripture

- Ps. 63:1–8
- Psalm 145
- Psalm 18 (selections)

How Differently We See
God's Characteristics

Using the examples provided, look up the Scripture passages and find a word or phrase that fits each grouping.

Ex. 3:13–14 (I am) _____

Deut. 32:18 (mother) _____

Ps. 7:8 (judge) _____

Ps.18:2 (rock, fortress, shield) _____

Ps. 23:1 (shepherd) _____

Ps. 61:3–4 (refuge, tower, shelter) _____

Ps. 68:5 (father) _____

Ps. 84:11 (sun, shield, protector) _____

Song of Sol. 2:1 (rose, lily) _____

Isa. 42:14 (woman in labor) _____

Isa. 64:8 (potter) _____

Isa. 66:13 (mother) _____

Matt. 3:16 (dove) _____

Matt. 6:9 (father) _____

2 Cor. 3:17 (Spirit) _____

2 Cor. 5:18 (friend) _____

1 John 4:8 (love) _____

Rev. 15:3 (King) _____

When you are finished, choose the one characteristic that you were the most comfortable with and the one characteristic you were the least comfortable with.

How do you see yourself *in relation* to the images you have of God (e.g., potter/clay; mother/child; king/subject; judge/sinner; rose or lily/admirer; bread/hungry; water/thirsty)?

Write down all the names you use most often when speaking of or to God. Circle the one or two that represent your true feelings.

"Journal" about the characteristics inherent in that name.

Come back together as a total group and discuss the characteristics of God that seem to surface (e.g., all-loving, forgiving, near, unchangeable).

Suddenly one day
It happened.
    I stood there in the crowd
    Cursing its density and anonymity,
    Angry that my feet had been stepped on
    And no one stopped to ask my pardon . . .

Then it hit me.
    I felt the life flowing out of me
    Into the bodies around me,
    And their life flowing into mine.
        I looked into faces for the first time,
        Realizing that I was not only myself,
        But I was a part of them as well.
        They and I were expressions of the same
            force—
        Life,
        Coming from somewhere,
        Housed in these bodies,
        Looking out of these eyes . . .

            And then I recognized them—
            These were the faces of God!

An invisible God
Is a very handy kind to have.
    I can't see him,
    And hopefully, the arrangement is mutual.
        It is like a small child
        Covering his face with his fingers
        And calling slyly,
        "You can't see me!"

But when that invisible God
Shines out of the eyes
Of the faces I meet every day,
    There is no game of hide-and-seek.
        We are here,
        You see me and I see you.
        The game is over,
            And a new awareness is upon us.
            There is no room for tricks now,
            Or little games of deceit.

And always about life there is this air of resolution,
Of things having been previously decided.
For I am as one
Who has seen the invisible God
In your face.

Retreat Theme

3

▮ Nudges from God

▮ What Is Discernment?

How can we know God's will for us? What is God's will? Frequently these questions come up in group discussions. As a youth, I remember well the purpose statement of our Westminster Fellowship: "to become such complete disciples of Christ that we will discover God's will for our lives and do it." Wow! Awesome, isn't it? And for youth at that! Of course, as adults, we are still trying to discover God's will.

Nowadays the word is *discernment*. How do I discern God's will? Or, what does God want me to do? These ponderings speak to everyone, whether young or old, lay or clergy, because they can relate to:

- one's sense of call (vocationally)
- the process of decision making (what I am being called to do)
- identification of gifts of ministry (in any locale)
- fulfilling a ministry within the church (elders, deacons, etc.)
- the desire to sense direction in one's life.

There have been many ways to discern. For our purposes, we will use the following statement:

Discernment is developing a habitual way of listening to God.[16]

What this means is that we are not asking God to give us a Damascus road event. Instead, we are willing to be content with developing a patient and listening path. Some of the signposts on the journey will raise questions such as: *How will I know this is of God?* The answer is another question: *Does it draw me toward God or not?*

Answering these questions helps us to uncover God's nudgings in our lives. These nudgings can relate to: uncovering gifts; the issue of "call" or decision making; discovery, vision, or seeing; understanding; and awareness—all of which are forms of the root word *discern*.

▮ Suggested Activities

1. A Moment of Grace

Write a sentence about a moment of grace that you experienced during the past week or so by responding to the following question: How was God present to you through another person? (Observe being touched through joy, pain, or revelation.) Ask people to share if they choose. When everyone is finished, note that these are ways in which we, in turn, minister to others. Ask: When have you felt that you have been a similar instrument for someone?

2. Choices—and Judging What's Important

Plain and Simple: A Woman's Journey to the Amish[17] is an excellent portrayal of values and priorities, especially pages 5–8 (choices); 24–25 (the faceless dolls); 48–51 (time, the sacred, and the everyday); 82–83 (the elegant dinner party: what I do vs. who I am); 126 ("not doing"); and 129–130 (story of the grandfather). Read aloud portions of this book to the group as they ponder what's important.

Discuss how you can be a spiritual friend to someone else without giving advice.

3. What Is Your Prayer?

Post the following passages:

1 Cor. 12:4–7 (gifts)
Psalm 42 (longing for God)
Psalm 25 (teach me your paths)
Ps. 4:1 (answer me!)
Psalm 130 (I cry to you; I wait for you)
Ex. 30:15–20 (choose this day)
Jer. 6:16 (looking for the right way)

Ask the participants to silently read all the passages and then choose one that seems right for them at this time in their life. Ask participants to spend some quiet time with that passage, then write a prayer that comes to them from reading the Word. Ask: What *is* your prayer?

4. Acknowledging Gifts

a. How I See Myself

Think for a moment about the gifts you have and how you see yourself. Make note of

- things you enjoy and from which you get deep satisfaction
- places where you feel you have been used or needed or blessed in a special way
- talents that have been appreciated
- service that has been inconspicuous or obvious, easy or difficult
- whatever has sparked a place within that says, "I feel that I am giving my best when I do this."

b. How Others See Me

Ask the participants to get into groups of five or six (the larger the group, the more feedback). In a special journal booklet (approximately three pages, folded or stapled) with a cover that each person has made or has been given, ask them to write their name at the top of the first five to six pages. Ask them to pass the booklet to the person on their right who will then write down the gifts he or she sees in the person whose name is printed on the page. Allow about five minutes for each "turn," then ask that the books continue to be passed to the right, until each person has his or her own book with input from everyone in the group.

When all groups have finished, ask the participants to find two people who were not in their small group and share any confirmations or surprises. Allow anyone who is uncomfortable to pass on this activity. (Most people, however, will be awed by this experience and eager to talk about their discoveries and affirmations.)

c. Quiet Time/Free Time

Instruct the participants to go for a walk, sit by a fire, look at the water, mountains, or other work of nature, or curl up in a chair. They should feel comfortable, so they can listen to what might come in the silence.

d. Read, Reflect, and Respond

Read the prayer found in Eph. 3:14–21. Sit for a moment in silence and then read it again. Then tell the participants to jot down any response the words in this passage trigger for them. Next, ask them to reflect on how things come together for them; that is, how they see themselves, how others see them, how the Scripture speaks to them. Then ask them to respond in their journals to the following:

How does God seem to be calling you or nudging you at this time for your own growth?

What indications do you have it is God?

Then ask them to express their responses through writing (poem, prayer, song, prose) or drawing. (Provide newsprint and large crayons or markers for this activity.) Tell the participants that they may choose to bring their expressions to the closing worship, feeling free to share it or not to share it.

5. How Do I Minister Best?

"Awakening the Minister Within," on pages 121–127, addresses the subject of *lay* ministry and helps to define the kinds of service or callings that one may have. Readers are encouraged to see if they can identify their particular kind of ministry from the following categories: Listener, Witness, Artist, Lover of God, Prophet, Liberator, Friend, Healer, Nurturer, Reconciler, Host/Hostess, Sparkplug, Manager, Servant/Laborer, Builder, and Shepherd. If you are having a retreat for officers and wish to use this concept, you can adapt the categories to fit the particular group. (One retreat group chose eight categories of their own for people to identify with: organizer–manager, idea person–sparkplug, host-hostess, healer–comforter, shepherd, nurturer–teacher, artist–creator, and listener–friend.)

Put the name of each form of ministry at the top of a piece of newsprint, along with an agreed-upon definition of each term. Post these around the room.

Ask the participants to read "Awakening the Minister Within" on pages 121–127. Then ask them to choose the forms that match their "sense of gift or call" the most and the ones that match it the least. Asking them the following question may be helpful: "How do you seem to minister best in sharing the 'Good News'?"

6. Seeing the Lord

Distribute a copy of "On Seeing the Lord" on pages 128–131. Ask the participants for general impressions.

7. Spiritual Friendship

Discuss the meaning of spiritual friendship and spiritual direction. Perhaps some may feel called to this form of spiritual discipline, either individually or with a small group. See Tilden Edwards' book *Spiritual Friend*,[18] which gives the background of the practice, as well as some information on seeking such a friend and being a friend. Although not well-established in Protestant circles, it is gaining acceptance as a valuable aid in spiritual nurture.

Group spiritual direction is also gaining in interest. See *Group Spiritual Direction: Community for Discernment*, by Rose Mary Dougherty.[19]

8. On Skills and Gifts

Use Parker Palmer's book *The Active Life*,[20] noting especially chapter 4, "The Woodcarver." The chapter, which is based on the title of a poem by Chuang Tzu, contains rich discussion material.[21]

In *The Active Life*, Palmer writes,

Discerning our native gifts is difficult for many reasons. We live in a culture that tells us there is no such thing as a gift, that we must earn or make everything we get. . . . But the most subtle barrier to the discernment of our native gifts is in the gifts themselves: They are so central to us, so integral to who we are, that we take them for granted and are often utterly unaware of the mastery they give us.

The skills we are most aware of possessing are often those we have acquired only through long hours of study and practice, at considerable financial or personal cost. Precisely because these skills once cost us effort to acquire, and still cost us effort to employ, we are acutely aware of owning them. Ironically, these self-conscious skills are often

not our leading strengths; if they were, they would not be so effortful. But they are the strengths upon which we sometimes build our identities and our careers. . . .

Our tendency to identify ourselves with our acquired skills rather than our natural gifts is one of the less desirable habits of the ego.[22]

After reading this aloud to the group, discuss the issue of natural gifts and skills by asking,

- What were the woodcarver's gifts and skills?
- What are your gifts and skills?
- How do you affirm them? blend them?
- How much is *doing* and how much is *being*?
- What is the difference?

9. Suggestion of Music for a Closing Worship

Use "He Has Anointed Me" on one of two tapes from *Intermissions: Song–Meditations for Personal and Communal Prayer*.[23] About ten minutes long, this music has the spoken word of Scripture and prayer interspersed with the music. Copy permission is given with the prayer services. The Scriptures used here are as follows: Jer. 1:4–8; Isa. 42:1, 6; and Matt. 25:35–36, 40.

10. Suggestion of Body Prayer for Worship

The following makes an excellent closing/benediction (see also pages 22–26 for instructions):

I am a delight to God my Creator
I am embraced by Christ Jesus the Son
I am a masterpiece-in-the-making of God's creative Holy Spirit.

11. Discerning Our Way

These are several ways to test our decision-making process. The following approaches are based on forms of discernment recommended by St. Ignatius.

- Imagine you are about to die. Looking back, what decision would you want to have made?
- Picture yourself at the Last Judgment, standing before this loving God. Again, what do you hope you have decided?
- You are approached by someone you care very much about. You are asked to help make the same decision for them. What would you say?

Ask the participants to write about a difficult situation they are currently experiencing.

Next, ask them to state how they feel God is leading them in this issue and/or decision. Allow for some quiet time.

John of the Cross[24] suggested another way to test our decision making.

He recommended that we bring ourselves into the presence of God—that we put away our efforts to think about the subject as well as any exploration of our feelings. We simply rest in God, hold the situation before God, and remain focused on the Almighty and not on the problem at hand. Then we wait. He maintains that if we are sufficiently open to what may come, a clear sense of what to do or where to turn will emerge.

This approach can be used as a time for intentional silence (see chapter 7). Ask the participants to reflect on what it was like to "rest in God" by writing or drawing in their journals.

12. Discerning God's Nudges

Read Psalm 139 from different translations. Then ask the following questions:

- What does it feel like to be known by God?
- How might this psalm be helpful in discerning God's nudges? See also Model B. Praying with Scripture (Psalm 139) on page 44.

13. Reflecting on Our Spiritual Growth

In order to gain a perspective on their present decision making and discernment, ask the participants to remember their earliest recollection of God. Then, from that point, ask them to design a graph that depicts the spiritual growth they have experienced, including the highs and lows. Ask them to note on the graph what the highs, lows, and plateaus represent.

After they are finished, ask them to reflect on their design and ponder the following:

- What are the common threads?
- What was going on in your life at that time?
- When do you find it easiest to be in God's presence? in the good times? in the rough times?
- See if there is any recollection or insight that might help you with your decision making today.

Allow time for them to share in small groups.

14. Discerning One's Call

H. Richard Niebuhr explained the process of discerning one's call by using four subdivisions:

- the call to be a Christian (universal)
- the secret or private call (ongoing or sudden)
- the providential call (to use talents in vocation)
- the ecclesiastical call (clerical ordination)[25]

Divide the participants into four groups. Ask them to explore what these four subdivisions might mean for the church and what they might mean for each person. Ask the following questions:

- Is this a fair description?
- Can you come up with one of your own that you prefer more than the subdivisions that Niebuhr has developed?

15. Discerning God's Presence through Prayer

Share with the group the prayer on this page, which is based on the Lord's Prayer. You may do so by reading it aloud to the group or writing it on newsprint or chalkboard.

The Prayer of Abandonment*

Father,
I abandon myself into your hands;
do with me what you will.
Whatever you may do, I thank you;
I am ready for all, I accept all.
Let only your will be done in me,
and in all your creatures.

I wish no more than this,
O Lord.
Into your hand I commend my soul;
I offer it to you with all the love
of my heart,
for I love you, Lord,
and so need to give myself,
to surrender myself into your hands,
without reserve
and with boundless confidence.
For you are my Father.

*From Charles de Foucauld, "A Prayer of Abandonment," as cited in Henri J. M. Nouwen, *The Road to Daybreak* (New York: Doubleday, 1988), p. 121.

Ask the participants to spend some quiet time with this prayer. Say aloud the following: Pray this prayer and let it pray in you. Relax into it. Allow yourself to absorb the desire it expresses.

When the silence is over, use the following questions for reflection in your journal:

- Were you able to make this prayer your own? Why? Why not?
- How did you relate to the image of God as Father? Was this comforting or did it get in the way of how you "see" God?
- What would it mean for you to abandon yourself to God?
- How does God's will seem to relate to your will in this prayer? Is that comforting or discomforting?
- How might you surrender yourself to God?
- Dialogue with God, in drama outline, about your reactions to these thoughts.
- Write a sentence prayer of your own as a form of closure.

16. Discerning What God Is Asking

Ask for volunteers to read John 21:1–6 from several different translations. Then ask the following questions, pausing between each one to allow the participants enough time for reflection.

- How does God seem to be asking you to cast your net on the other side?
- How might God be dealing with you? inviting you? challenging you? loving you? hiding from you? just being there for you?
- How do you seem to be relating to God? Are you trusting? loving? resistant? hiding? challenging? inviting? just being there?

Sit with Jesus in the boat and let the feelings, impressions, and sensations wash over you. Then use crayons and paper to express your feelings.

If appropriate, the participants may want to share what is in their drawings.

Awakening the Minister Within

Who are the ministers in your church? The people of most congregations, if asked, would naturally name only the ordained clergy. It is a revelation to most laity that they are, according to scripture, *ministers,* as gifted and called by God to their own forms of ministry as any pastor.

Most laity think of the pastor as *the* minister, someone ordained. If the minister is doing the ministry of the church, what then are the laity doing? Most figure they are doing "volunteer work" or assisting the pastor in doing his or her ministry! I find few laity thinking of themselves as having either a "ministry" or a "calling" from God. These terms are used almost exclusively in reference to clergy.

Our usual language about ministers and ministry is not only unbiblical (see 1 Peter 2:9–10, 1 Cor. 12:4–11), but it reveals such constricting, disempowering categories that the laity and their God-given gifts for ministry are absolutely paralyzed. The laity are kept dysfunctional and spiritually undeveloped, and the clergy remain isolated and burnt-out. Christ holds another vision! It is absolutely thrilling to be part of a congregation where the members (laity and clergy together!) begin to encourage each other to claim their own unique Biblical identity of "minister," probe their gifts, and discern and unleash their ministries.

Obviously, it is not helpful to be clones of the ordained, understanding "minister" and "ministry" according to what pastors do. That is like wearing somebody else's shoes. Most lay-ministries are quite different from the preachers, taking place primarily where laity work as businessmen and women, teachers, homemakers, or taxi cab drivers. Unlike clergy who have traditionally well-defined roles and responsibilities, laity have few definitions to define themselves with as ministers and must find it through their creativity and openness to God.

The rest of this article is a kind of worksheet that can help laity (and clergy) think in some new ways about what kind of ministers they are. Here are sixteen "non-priestly" images of minister, along with reflection questions. Put on each identity one at a time like a pair of glasses through which to view yourself and your work for God. Which ones describe you the best? the least? As you ponder each minister identity below, ask yourself, "What is my personal style of ministering, of bringing God's "good news" to my corner of the world?" Before you lay down this article, see if you can name for yourself what kind of minister you are!

1. Minister as Listener

A listening heart hears the cries of God within and the cries of your neighbors in need. It lets the world into your soul and enables you to step into the shoes of others. When you listen, others feel honored and upheld; you build trust and open relationships. Your plans do not become idols, because they are molded by your attentiveness to God and others on how forceful or tender to be, how fast to move, what directions to pursue. Listening ministers are often thinkers or contemplatives whose quiet gift is the measured and deep wisdom that comes from silent places.

Questions. In what ways are you a listening minister? How might you listen more deeply to those in your workplace, home, church, or world?

2. Minister as Witness

Jesus said, "You shall be my witnesses . . . to the end of the earth" (Acts 1:8). Witnessing is the action of every Christian who expresses the "good news" of Christ through word or deed, anything from a welcoming smile, to the contagious joy that comes from a changed life, to the silent witness of a compassionate act, to more traditional verbal expressions of evangelism. Christians with the gift of words take on this ministry the most fully as preachers, evangelists, or poets for Christ. When Christians find their own humble ways to speak of how God works in their lives, their witness spiritually empowers their church companions, and gives hope to those who have yet to be changed by God's grace.

Questions. In what ways do your words, actions, or attitudes witness to the "good news" of Christ?

3. Minister as Artist

Jesus says, "Whoever believes in me . . . streams of living water will flow from within him [or her]" (John 7:38). This is a wonderful image of expression: streams of living water pouring out of you! Ministry for Christ is a profound act of expression, of unleashing your creativity, your gifts, your "streams of living water" for God. When we do ministry with God, we become co-artists with God, fashioning a more beautiful world with our minds, hearts, hands, voice, or body. God calls you to express yourself simply, humbly, authentically, being faithful to your particular passions, concerns, and ways of ministering.

Questions. How do you, like an artist, express your gifts for God? How might you do that more fully?

4. Minister as Lover

Ministry is expressing love. "If I give away all that I have, if I give my body to be burned, but have not love, I gain nothing" (1 Cor. 13:3). Ministry must always be motivated by love, even in conflicted situations. The minister is a conduit of God's radical love that includes oppressed and oppressor, poor and rich, friend and foe. The minister is God's lover taking delight in life and in others, feeling intensely committed to personal relationships, or to expansive compassion that wants to hold the earth.

Questions. In what ways are you a lover for God? What is your personal style of showing love? How might you let the lover within you blossom more?

5. Minister as Prophet

The prophet is the challenger who is uncomfortably honest and says, "No" when the crowd says, "Yes." The prophet is the questioner, reformer, disturber of old patterns, the one who causes us to look candidly at ourselves, our personal relationships, or our society, and calls us out of our sin or slumber. The prophet is also the Dreamer, holding up the dream of a renewed, God-centered life. Sometimes "a voice crying out in the wilderness," the prophet feels the divine hunger for human transformation and truthful living (Jer. 1:10).

Questions. In what areas of your life are you a prophet for God? How might you be more prophetic in your relationships, workplace, or church?

6. Minister as Liberator

This one, like Moses leading the Israelite slaves out of Egypt, hungers to offer freedom to those imprisoned by poverty, illiteracy, racial oppression, or unjust political/economic structures. The liberator works for justice and decency, seeking to remove obstacles that crush or hold back the potential of people.

Questions. In what ways do you act as a liberator for others in your workplace and world? How do you help people step out of their prisons and move ahead?

7. Minister as Friend

Here is the one who visits, phones, holds hands, or writes notes, who simply and humbly offers companionship, walking with others through their joy and suffering. The friend looks beneath the masks of wealth, knowledge, sex, race, or spiritual development, and sees the equality of souls, and the deep integrity and beauty of each person's journey. There is no hierarchy of caring, no prophetic arrogance, no authoritarian teaching, no judgments about who is "important" or "more deserving of love." Here is an unconventional understanding of authority: the last is first; we wash each other's feet (John 15:15).

Questions. In what ways are you a friend to others? How might you be more of a friend to your boss, employees, or neighbors?

8. Minister as Healer

This minister is the comforter, the forgiver, the one who offers deep acceptance that heals, the one who gets people back on their feet. You can help heal physically or spiritually with your hands, words, love, or prayers. Everywhere we look, we see griefs, hurts, broken human beings, failed relationships all needing healing.

The healer is a "redeemer" of the old, bringing it back to life and wholeness. Healers themselves are wounded, but can use their wounds to guide their caring of others as "wounded healers."

Questions. In what ways do you serve as a healer for others, and/or how might you, be more so?

9. Minister as Nurturer

This is the one who lovingly draws out the best in others, a facilitator, a patron of people's gifts who assists them to unfurl their wings, and be all that God intended. You create a safe, enabling environment to awaken the potential and purpose of others through teaching, parenting, coaching, complimenting, and creating opportunities.

Questions. How do you nurture others? How might you be more so at work, home, school, church, or world?

10. Minister as Reconciler

This minister seeks to build bridges between people and bring them together. A peacemaker, a community builder, a negotiator, this minister helps people walk in another's shoes, find common ground with loved ones, neighbors, or enemies, and come to an understanding between those who differ culturally, racially, sexually, doctrinally, or in years. He/she is a healer of conflict and division, and hungers to attain the harmonious and interdependent Body of Christ.

Questions. How do you act as a reconciler or bridgemaker in your home, workplace, or church?

11. Minister as Host/Hostess

This minister offers hospitality, welcomes the stranger, opens his or her home, and provides warmth and shelter. This minister makes people feel "at home" and provides an environment where people can let down, relax, and be themselves. Either by welcoming a stranger into a new group, or providing a weary traveler a bed to sleep in at night, or by offering one's own church as "sanctuary" to refugees, this minister cares for Christ in the stranger.

Questions. How do you welcome the stranger? What are your ways of being a host/hostess for God?

12. Minister as Sparkplug

This minister is a catalyst of new things, a visionary, an idea person, one who builds fires under people and gets things moving. A fearless optimist who sees and proposes what God can make possible. He/she is always planting seeds, sowing leaven, and getting people thinking and growing. This minister "thinks big," stretches people's imaginations, and offers others an energy that *is* contagious and creative.

Questions. What are your ways of being a "sparkplug" for God in your relationships, workplace, [or] church?

13. Minister as Manager

Organizing and harnessing people's energies, this minister gets people working together for God productively and efficiently. He/she makes teamwork happen, valuing each contribution and respectfully managing his or her limits and potential. The manager molds and oversees cooperative efforts and is able to develop guidelines, policies, or methods in the workplace, home, and church that ensure smooth coordination and fruitful group activity.

Questions. How are you a sensitive manager for Christ with your family, your neighborhood, your church, or your fellow workers?

14. Minister as Servant/Laborer

Here is the worker for Christ who serves on committees, work parties, and task forces who "enjoys getting things done." Jesus said, "I chose you . . . that you should go and bear fruit . . . " (John 15:16). This minister, not necessarily a leader-type, enjoys being a fruitful laborer for God, "doing my part" in a larger group that is seeking to express the healing and love of God to the world.

Questions. In what ways do you "get things done" for God? How are you a fruitful laborer for God?

15. Minister as Builder

This is one who intentionally seeks to build a better world: better housing, new programs, new policies, new relationships.

Some build with their hands, cooking, cleaning, renovating. Others use their engineering, business, or interpersonal skills to organize neighborhood or family activities, or larger business or political ventures of compassion. We each have our way to help to build God's new heaven and earth.

Questions. In what ways are you a builder of a better world for God? How have you been doing this lately?

16. Minister as Shepherd

God gives each of us clergy and laity, a certain "congregation" to care for: a personal network of family, friends, co-workers, maybe some elderly folks in a nursing home, street people in our city's soup kitchen. This [group] may not be outwardly defined, but it is the group that God calls you to love, pray for, and quietly look after.

Questions. Which people has God put in your life to care for? Who makes up your congregation?

Perhaps most all of these identities speak to you in some way. Review the list and choose two that you feel best describe your style of ministering. What next steps might you take to deepen or expand your approaches to ministry? Choose two other identities to which you feel attracted but need to develop more in yourself. What might you do to strengthen these in your workplace, relationships, home, or world? Next, choose the two identities that seem *least* descriptive of you. Though they

may be, for the most part, "not your style," what might you take from them to round out the way you try to minister? Lastly, what new images come to mind that might more accurately describe your unique way of ministering to others in Christ's name?

May God bless your journey and your ministry!

Ron Farr, "Awakening the Minister Within," *Faith at Work*, May/June 1991, pp. 8–9, 14. Ron Farr, a UCC copastor with his wife, Patty, in Watertown, N.Y., is a writer, small group trainer, retreat leader, and director of the Laity Empowerment Project, which trains local church leadership teams to empower their churches through two core curricula, *Unwrapping Our Gifts* and *Unleashing Our Weekday Ministries*. This article was taken from the latter core curriculum. For more information, call 315-583-5821. Used by permission.

On Seeing the Lord

Shame on you! you . . .
who have no eyes for the work of
    the LORD
and never see the things he
    has done.
                    —Isa. 5:11–12 (NEB)

Our relationship with God can be compared to other human relationships, and the Bible is filled with such images. God is like our parent, our spouse, our friend. Yet our involvement with God is different because the invisible God is far greater than we can even begin to comprehend.

In our human commitments, it almost goes without saying that we must see others in order to relate to them. Even if we do not actually see persons with our eyes, we may hear them on the telephone or receive letters from them through the mail. We must in some way experience and acknowledge their presence. When we fail to do this, no relationship can develop. A typical example of failure is when we "look over the head of a child" without really noticing his or her presence. Children have a way of getting our attention with words such as "Mommy, you are not listening to me."

We usually do not see God with our eyes, hear God with our ears, or get a letter from God. Therefore, we must develop other senses with which to "see" the presence of God in our lives and in events in the world. We can reflect on our friendships, jobs, church involvement, and conflicts and sufferings. After reflecting upon and sorting out these aspects of our life, we must then move on to the deeper questions: Where is God in all this? Where in my life do I encounter God most powerfully? Where is the Lord at work bringing peace out of turmoil? How does God want me to relate to this person? How might God want me to grow in my feelings about myself? What are my gifts and how can I use them for others? Does this or that decision fit with God's will for my life? How is God working for justice and peace in the larger world, and how can I be involved? These are fundamental questions about the meaning of our lives, and we must be intentional in asking them.

In order to grow spiritually, it is necessary for us to grow in our relationship with God. To do that, we must first see God acting in our everyday situations. We must look and we must listen if we are to develop an awareness of God and our own sensitivity to the divine mystery. God is present not only in certain selected compartments of our lives but also at the deepest level of all life.

As the apostle Paul said, "Indeed [God] is not far from each of us. For in him we live and move and have our being" (Acts 17:27–28, NRSV). No area of our life is beyond the concern of God.

A misconception that may prevent us from seeing God is the idea that God comes to us primarily in big splashy ways. We wish for a dream that will give specific directions or a clear sign from heaven. Chances are God is not going to reveal the Spirit's presence in that way. The trick is: *Think small!* Look for God in what is close to you—in the unusual insight of a child in your church school class, in the prayers of two or three teachers together, in an apology from someone for an unintended hurt, in the beauty of a flower, in the rich melody of a song. Look for God in the ordinary. *Think small.*

A specific way to become more intentional about seeing God and developing our sensitivity to God's action is to spend time in reflection at the end of each day. Before you go to sleep, ask yourself, Where did I see God today? Another way of asking the question is, Where was the joy and where was the turmoil? Then spend a few minutes in prayer talking with God about it.

As we try to become more aware of God, our prayers will have more content. Then we will say, Thank you, Lord, for doing that; I don't understand why this is happening; I am angry about that; or Help me with this. If we are saying the same thing over and over in our personal prayers, it may be because we have not noticed God's acting in our lives. Friends who spend quality time together have lots to talk about. To develop our spirituality, then, the starting point is simply to see God.

The second thing that will help us to grow in our spiritual life is to tell someone about our experiences. We need to share what God is doing and how that relationship is developing. Somewhere among our Christian friendships and within the Christian community, this sharing needs to happen. Why is this important?

When we have an experience of God, we may tend to discount it. We may write it off with various excuses: I thought God was telling me something in the middle of the night, but it must have been that pizza I ate at bedtime. I think I would like to go back to college, but I am probably too old. I would like to be chairperson of that committee, but I don't have the gifts. I should spend more time with my spouse, but I am too busy.

However, when we share an insight, a burden, or a possibility with other Christians, they may affirm it for us: Yes, you'd be good at that! Did you call the college for an application? Perhaps you are coming to realize that you ought to deal with that broken relationship before anything else.

We need to be affirmed in our experiences of God's will. Again, God's word to us is not always easy to understand. Things are not always clearly defined. Often we must choose between two apparent goods, and we need the help of others to discern God's will. They can help us reflect on and clarify the experience. For example, after the death of her spouse, one woman told a friend that God must have been angry with her to allow such a thing to happen. She had misinterpreted the event of her husband's death and she needed a loving friend to help her come to a clearer understanding. In discerning God's will, it is essential to

remember that the Scriptures are our starting point. God does not call us to do something that is against God's own law or the teachings and example of Jesus.

By sharing with others our high points with God, we can ensure they will be there to recall them to us when our faith is shaky, and we can do the same for them. We can remind them: I know you are feeling low now, but remember how God led you through that other tough time? High experiences of God become our touchstones. When we are in "dry times of the soul," we can reach back into our past and recall when God was present. This restores hope.

When we share our faith experiences together, it nurtures the faith of each person. Collectively there is much more going on than singly. We see that God really is a great power among us, and it gives us cause

for celebration and thanksgiving. We become aware of new ways to look for God's presence.

Our growth in the life of faith would be enriched if we were more intentional about sharing our experiences of God with one another. Find one other person with whom you meet periodically as a "spiritual friend." Begin each Christian education or church school teacher's meeting by providing time for people to talk about the question, Where have I seen God in my life since the last meeting? The sharing could be done within the whole group or one on one. If every meeting and study group in your church were to begin with such a sharing time, members would come to see that it is time well spent!

If some are uncomfortable with this at first, an easy way to start is to pass out paper and pencils and ask them to make notes about experiences with God.

After all are finished, encourage those who are willing to share to do so, but always respect a person's privacy. Even if they do not share aloud, just identifying and writing about God's presence can be an important first step. Further, knowing that the same question will be reflected upon at the next meeting will increase awareness of God in the intervening time. Noticing God and sharing that awareness together in the Christian community is an important first step in our spiritual development, in our growing ability to "see the Lord."

Nancy Regensburger, "On Seeing the Lord," *Alert,* Nov 1991, pp. 15–16. Nancy Regensburger is a resident of Vassar, Michigan. She is an educator, theologian, and freelance writer.

Retreat Theme

4

■ Spiritual Disciplines for the Stressed-Out

This retreat is intended to be an introduction to some of the spiritual disciplines that might be fresh and new and welcome to those who feel "stressed-out." The emphasis is on the different ways we can be open to God's presence. Because most of the ideas presented below are described elsewhere in this handbook, what follows are suggestions to illustrate how they might be assembled as a *"Taste and See"* retreat.

1. *Suggested Handouts*—Journals, a Bibliography, and "Balance, Discipline, and Illumination" found in chapter 9 on page 151.

2. *Suggested Music*—Have music playing (like the extended version of "Jesu, Joy of Man's Desiring") and appropriate posters on the walls when people arrive.

3. *Opening*—Open with "Prayer for a Busy Day" on page 144.

4. *Introduction*—In a relaxed manner, talk about our need for rest and re-treating ourselves. Read Mark 6:30–32. Tell the story of the hermit (see page 13), or another similar story.

5. *Beginning the Activity*—Ask them to ponder the following questions, and write their thoughts in their journals. Assure them that no one will see what they write, nor will they have to share it.

- What is going on in your life right now?
- What would you like to be different?
- Where is God in all of this?

When everyone has finished, discuss the value of journaling: from life, from dreams, from Scripture, as responses to guided meditation, and so forth. Depending on the amount of time available, explore with the participants how they feel about "journaling." Assure them that if they are new to "journaling," that they will more than likely feel more comfortable with the process by the end of the retreat.

6. *Setting the Expectations*—Review the fact that there are no expectations for retreat "experiences." Emphasize their willingness to relax into the opportunities and be open. Use this time to encourage the group to establish their own "space" at home: a time—a place—a quiet environment without any distractions.

7. *Setting the Theme*—Remind the group that they are here because they are "stressed-out," but that this is not a stress management course! Instead, they will be offered some "windows" that may be useful in their daily lives. Invite the participants to become aware and attentive by appreciating small things, letting go of all the baggage they brought with them (they can decide what that might be), and focusing on being available to God's presence.

▌ Suggested Activities

The following suggested activities do not need to be done in the order given, and certainly not without a break after each! Remember that a change of pace is helpful, as well as allowing time to digest what is being offered. Some of these activities are slight variations of others, so a choice will need to be made. Don't try to offer everything!

Most important of all, remember that most of these activities call for a period of silence. This is *extremely* important. Be careful not to plan too much. Do fewer things in a relaxed manner. Don't give the participants spiritual indigestion!

1. Body Prayer/Guided Relaxation

Use any of the body prayers on pages 25–26, or make up your own. It is best to begin with simple activities—things that the participants can do while sitting or movements that have prayer thoughts associated with them, so that the movements are not associated with "exercise."

2. Breath Prayer

See Model A. Breath Prayer from Scripture (Psalm 62:1) on page 42 or Model G. The Jesus Prayer on page 59. Consider asking the participants to do the following:

- Notice their breathing. Follow it. Count their breaths.
- Inhale God's Spirit, and then exhale what seems not to be of God.

3. Centering Words

This involves selecting a sacred word, which helps focus one's thoughts when they begin to wander, then gradually finding that perhaps even the word disappears as one moves into deep inner spaces of divine communion. Centering practices include simple silence as well as using a word or phrase or chant to assist one in moving into the deeper silence. Use a word in connection with breathing. Ask the participants to let a word rise within that seems right during the period of silence, such as the following: God, alleluia, peace, shalom, and so forth. Encourage them to use whatever word may come to their minds. Tell them that whenever their mind begins to stray, gently lead it back to focusing on that particular word.

4. Praying with Scripture

Use Model B. Praying with Scripture (Psalm 139) on page 44.

5. Seeing God in the Everyday and the Ordinary Things of Life

Use Model M. Seeing God in the Ordinary on pages 80–81. This is a good way to help the participants realize that they need not separate God from the rest of life!

6. Meditation

Use the Gelineau Psalms tape, Psalm 23 (listed as Psalm 22 in the Septuagint numbering). This tape may be used as a simple meditation, followed by silence. Participants may also create a psalm and write it in their journals (see Retreat Theme 1. Simple Gifts, pages 86–106).

7. Silence and Reflection

After reviewing the background material in Model L. Sound and Silence, use music such as:

- a tape of Tibetan bells (be careful these are not jarring versions!)
- Gregorian chants
- Other selections are found in chapter 10

Whatever is chosen, make sure that it leads one into a period of silence and reflection, either through the sound, the repetition of the words, or a combination of these. Prepare reflection questions for journaling.

8. Explore Dialogue with Jesus

Use Model F. Bar-timaeus/Bat-timaeus (see pages 57–58). This is usually an excellent exercise for women—being able to hear the feminine version puts them really "in the picture"!

9. Use Scripture

Use a passage of Scripture (e.g., Eph. 3:14–21 and John 14:12–13) and personalize it by changing the pronouns to the first person singular, or if someone is speaking, have them address the participant by name. Or you may want to personalize a hymn by changing the pronouns in the same way (e.g., Dear Lord and [Creator] of [humankind], forgive *my* foolish ways, etc.).

10. Write a Letter to God

See Fynn's *Mister God, This is Anna* (especially pp. 38–40, 155–156, 169–171) and Alice Walker's *The Color Purple* (especially pp. 176–179) for examples. Or ask the participants to write a prayer, being honest and open.

11. Put Yourself in the Scene

See Model I. The Rich Young Ruler (pages 63–64). Ask the participants to journal about any priority in life that might separate them from their desire for God.

12. Learn a Chant

"Ubi caritas" from Taizé (on several tapes) is lovely to do as a group. The words mean, "Where love and charity are, there is God." This can be used as a benediction, as well as several others from the Shalem tape (see chapter 10).

13. Write a Letter from God to Yourself

Ask the participants to begin a letter in the following way: "Dear [*Your name*]," and end with "Love, God." Encourage them to let it flow naturally—to just begin. When they are finished, ask them to prayerfully and silently read the letter. Then ask them to reflect on the following questions:

- What longings does the letter stir within you?
- Is there evidence of any misconceptions you might have about God?
- Do you see any attributes of God that you might have forgotten?
- Is there a path that seems to unfold for you at this time?

Retreat Theme

5

▮ Earthen Vessels

This retreat can focus on several aspects: the potter/creator, the clay/us, and the treasure in the earthen vessel/Christ. The possibilities for developing this theme are almost limitless.

If you have access to some earthen pots, or know of someone who collects them, this would be an excellent way to gather together a focal point for your retreat. They can be used for the center of your meeting area, or worship area, and for one of the suggested activities.

▮ Suggested Activities

1. Icebreaker

Go around and share two things about yourself that the others in the group may not know.

Share with the person next to you what this retreat means to you.

Introduction to retreat—see chapter 5, "Openers" (page 13) and other activities in chapter 6 (page 27).

Ask the participants to write in their journals (which you have prepared for them) their thoughts to the following statements:

- "Where I am . . ."
- "Where I want to be . . ."

2. Guided Relaxation

a. Body Prayer

(*Read very slowly*)

Hands out in front . . . palms up . . . open, open to truth

Round them out like a bowl, raise up to lips . . . drink

Raise up again and pour over your head.

Reach up . . . and then slowly . . . bend down.

With hands on hips, express defiance . . .

Resistance . . . twisting and turning or whatever comes.

Note the message this conveys and how it feels.

Then bend down . . . in submission, letting go of self.

Gradually bring body back to standing position.

Put arms out to the side, palms down— letting go of anything and everything.

Then turn them up . . . opening to what they might receive.

Keep them there while you:

Turn head to the left . . . with the right ear up . . . listen . . .

then to the right with left ear up . . . listen.

Then look straight ahead . . . focus . . . notice.

Notice weight of hands/arms at this point.

Now bring them in as a cup, then as a prayer posture.

Breathe in what is of God/allow yourself to exhale all that is not of God.

When you feel ready, slowly take your seat.

b. Deep Breathing

The deep cavity in the body holds air, breath, God's spirit, God's healing light. Exhale, see the negative flowing out. Inhale, feel God's positive energy, love, light entering. Feel the air around you . . . the floor beneath you, . . . the fluids circulating in your body . . . any tense spots or soreness. Pay attention to the rhythm of your body and how it is perfectly made to function.

3. Filling Our Own Cups

In keeping with the above relaxation, speak to the group about the human tendency to keep accumulating things without emptying. Usually our homes acquire enough to fill the space. We leave things lying around for that "homey" look. Our desks are cluttered, and we look busy. Our heads are full of agendas. But how do we nurture ourselves from our own cups? Are we trying to fill our own cups?

First, we must face the fact that our own cups are never empty. But, what is this emptying process? Perhaps letting go of something. Maybe peeling away a protective layer. Maybe allowing something to be less important. For most of us it means the risk of feeling, then fearing being empty or even looking empty, or naked, or maybe appearing unacceptable, unprepared, unattractive . . . whatever.

Read aloud 2 Cor. 4:7, after having mentioned passages from Genesis, Isaiah, or Jeremiah that refer to God's marvelous creation. After reading the passage from 2 Corinthians, explain that even though we are God's wonderful creation, we also have a treasure (Christ) that should be within us. How can we put something into a cup that is already full to brimming over?

Ask each participant to hold their clay pot and reflect on what they need to give up or empty in order to be filled.

4. "Abba Father"

Listen to the song and then sing the chorus.[26] Use it at different times during the retreat. Another song that is extremely applicable here is "Earthen Vessels,"[27] by the same group.

5. "Genesis from Space"

Try to obtain a taped copy of "Genesis from Space"—when the Apollo astronauts read the story of Creation from the moon. It is very moving.

6. Hymns

Use a hymnbook to find hymns related to creation, creator, and clay vessels. Plan to use some of these during the times of worship. Here are a few examples:

- "God, You Spin the Whirling Planets"
- "God, Who Made the Earth and Heaven" (sung to the tune "All Through the Night")
- "Have Thine Own Way, Lord"
- "Creating God, your fingers trace"
- "Abba Father"
- "Earthen Vessels"

7. "Return to Gaia"

Play "Return to Gaia" from *Earth Mass,* by Paul Winter.[28] It is also known as *Missa Gaia.* (*Gaia* is the Greek word for "mother earth.") This passage is a dream fantasy from space, suggesting that the human is floating in space and looking down at the earth. Gradually, the awesomeness of the sight brings an intense longing that slowly brings one closer and closer to "home." The ethereal sounds at the beginning (played by the soprano saxophone) are joined by the organ and crescendos as one comes closer to "home." Then a sudden silence, which is followed by the sound of a loon welcoming one home. This piece can be played in worship that is centered around the Creator and creation. We are part of this earth, this creation that God pronounced good. Let us rejoice and be glad in it!

8. *Prayer from St. Irenaeus*

Read aloud the prayer that appears below. Irenaeus lived in the second century and was a bishop of Lyons, Gaul. He wrote sophisticated discourses compared to other early Christian writers, and was a champion of free will.

It is not thou that shapest God,
It is God that shapest thee.
If then thou art the work of God,
await the hand of the artist who does
    all things in due season.
Offer him thy heart,
soft and tractable, and keep the form
    in which the artist has fashioned thee.
Let thy clay be moist,
lest thou grow hard
    and lose the imprint of his fingers.

(Prayer from St. Irenaeus)

Ask the participants to express what thoughts they have about the following questions by writing them in their journals.

- What does this prayer say about God? about praying? about me?
- What questions does it raise for me?

Allow time to share in small groups Scripture that relates to this prayer.

Note: You may want to share with the group that this prayer relates to the following passage:

> Just as clay is in the potter's hands
>   for him to shape as he pleases,
> so we are in the hands of our
>   Creator
>   for him to do with as he wishes.
> (Sirach 33:13)

9. 2 Corinthians 4

Using 2 Corinthians 4, ask the participants to write in their journal what it might mean for them to be a container (earthen vessel). Ask them to share what they have written in small groups.

10. *The Empty Vessel*

Behold, Lord, an empty vessel that needs to be filled. My Lord, fill it. I am weak in the faith; strengthen me. I am cold in love; warm me and make me fervent, that my love may go out to my neighbour. I do not have a strong and firm faith; at times I doubt and am unable to trust you altogether. O Lord, help me. Strengthen my faith and trust in you. In you I have sealed the treasure of all I have. I am poor; you are rich and came to be merciful to the poor. I am a sinner; you are upright. With me, there is an abundance of sin; in you is the fullness of righteousness. Therefore I will remain with you, of whom I can receive, but to whom I may not give.

(Martin Luther)[29]

11. Experience a Pot

This experience (also referred to as "pick-a-pot") requires the leader to have enough clay pots (earthen vessels) so that everyone can have one to "be with."

Place the vessels in a central place for viewing. Participants should carefully note that the vessels have different characteristics. Some may be lovely, unglazed and rough, or smooth. Others may have holes, lids or corks; beautiful, ornate designs, or simple designs; thin necks, so water cannot be quickly poured out; or handles, so they can be picked up easily.

Mention that sometimes people are like these vessels. They are warm or cool, easily grasped or attract attention, "bottled up" and "uptight," and on and on. Give the participants a few minutes to contemplate that idea and then ask them to pick one of the vessels. Each participant should find a place to just "be with" their earthen vessel for thirty to forty-five minutes. During that time, they should experience silence and write or draw in their journal about how they feel they are like the vessel or relate to the vessel they chose. Reflection questions might be as follows:

- How do you identify with the vessel? positively? negatively?
- How is it a symbol of your life and being?
- What is it saying to you?
- Conclude by writing a short summary sentence or prayer, just for you.

Another suggestion is to sketch it. (Many people remember the experience and wish they could remember the vessel a bit better.)

12. Psalm Reading

Use Psalms 148 and 139.

13. Bible Study

Read aloud Isa. 45:9–10 and Jer. 18:1–12 and ask the participants (in small groups) to do the following:

- Write a sentence or two summarizing the essence of the passage.
- Read the commentaries (already prepared as handouts by the leader) on these passages.
- As a group, write on newsprint any facts you found noteworthy or new to you. Share reactions as a group.

14. Creation

Obtain a self-hardening variety of clay in both gray and terra cotta. Give each participant a block and allow them to mingle and create at the same time.

This makes for a wonderfully pleasant afternoon. It can either be free form (with no directions), or you can ask them to mold something that represents a gift that they have received from God. The sharing is usually memorable. Whatever is made, no matter what it looks like, place each person's mold with the other vessels. Or, instead of using the original pots, place the new "creations" in the center for closing worship. In case they are not dry enough, come prepared with wax paper to place underneath them.

15. Julian of Norwich

Provide an opportunity for people to reflect on *Praying with Julian of Norwich*,[30] especially chapter 12. The meditation is called "We Are God's Work of Art," which is based on Eph. 2:10.

16. Have Thine Own Way

From a collection of slides, ask participants to select a slide that fits with a line of the hymn "Have Thine Own Way, Lord." This helps to incorporate their own experiences into the closing worship.

17. Guided Meditations

See Anthony de Mello's guided meditation on the sculptor in his book *Sadhana* (pages 81–82).[31] Someone makes a statue of you, you speak to it, you become it, and then Jesus walks into the room. It has much potential for silence and reflection, and different ways of seeing ourselves as the "creation."

See also "The Vessel" on this page. This guided meditation raises many thoughtful questions for reflection.

18. *Bring Many Names*

Sing *Bring Many Names*, words by Brian Wren and music by Donna Kasbohm. Hope Publishing Company, Carol Stream, IL 60188.

19. *Prayer of the Chalice*

Read aloud the "Prayer of the Chalice" on page 140.

The Vessel*

I ask God for a special kind of body
and get the one I have right now.
What thoughts and feelings do I have about
    this body?

We hear of saints who hated
or were neutral to their bodies.
What attitude is mine?
Where did I get it?

In the blueprint I have drawn up for my life
how does my body help or hinder?

If it could speak,
what would my body say about the
    blueprint?

My relationship with my body
powerfully affects my life for good or evil.
The finest way to heal,
or deepen, the relationship
is dialogue.

My body must be frank in expressing its
    resentments—
and its fears—of me.

I must be just as frank.

We keep at it till we are reconciled
and understand and love each other better.

We must then state explicitly
our expectations of each other.

Before we end the dialogue
I ask my body for a word of wisdom.

Scripture reveals my body's spirituality.
It says my body is God's temple,
the spirit's dwelling place.
What does that mean?

It further says our bodies are not ours but
    Christ's,
so he can say of me, "This is my body."
Again I wonder at the meaning of those
    words.

I see myself go through the actions of the
    day
(eating, washing, playing, sleeping)
with the consciousness
that my body is the home of the divine.

Or caring for it
as for the body of my beloved.

Finally I speak to God about my body
and listen as he speaks to me.

*From *Wellsprings*, by Anthony de Mello, pp. 23–24. Copyright © 1984 by Anthony de Mello, S.J. Used by permission of Doubleday, a division of Bantam Doubleday Dell Publishing Group, Inc.

Prayer of the Chalice*

Father, to You I raise my whole being,
— a vessel emptied of self. Accept, Lord,
this my emptiness, and so fill me with
Yourself — Your Light, Your Love, Your Life —
that these precious Gifts
may radiate through me and
overflow from the chalice of my heart
unto the hearts of all with whom
I come in contact this day
revealing unto them
the beauty of
Your Joy
and
Wholeness
the
Serenity
of Your Peace
which nothing can destroy

Amen.

—Frances Nuttall

*Source unknown.

"Spend" Your Summer Differently This Year!

Retreat Theme

6

▌ A Personal Retreat

When this time of year rolls around, we inevitably ask, "When (or where) are you going on vacation?" I was struck by the news item of a proposal to lengthen the vacation period to six weeks so that people can have more options at their disposal when "on leave" and also benefit from the added rest away from the job. We spend the year looking forward to vacations, only to return and begin the cycle all over again. So I am suggesting some common and uncommon ways to "spend" the whole summer. Pick a new one each week!

1. Get up earlier than usual one morning and go for *a walk* alone. Look and listen to the sights and sounds. Take *notice* of things you might normally overlook. Or, if you cannot go for a walk, rest in a comfortable chair near a window, or lie down for a nap, and turn on your senses instead of turning them off.

2. *Play* at something. Choose what you would most like to do, and do it. Treat yourself.

3. Get some kindergarten (big) crayons and a pad of paper. *Draw* a picture that reminds you of your childhood, in the same style you might have drawn then. Have fun doing it. Let the memories roll.

4. Browse among your old book collection and *reread* one that you enjoyed in the past. Try to find some new meanings in it this time.

5. *Soak your feet* in a pan of water while you read the daily paper or while you relax in a lawn chair.

6. *Phone or write* an old friend you have neglected. Make their day. It will make yours, too.

7. Spend one day *without* turning on the *television*. Think about the quality of life you would have if you had no electricity. Would it be better or worse?

8. Read Psalm 139 one verse at a time. Write down what each verse makes you think of—your concerns, your fears, your *thankfulness*, your wishes. Then *write* a psalm or poem of your own using those words you have written.

9. *Share a day,* or part of a day, with a person whom you suspect is lonely.

Prayer by a Sixteenth-Century Priest*

There is nothing I can give you
     which you have not got,
but there is much, very much,
     that, while I cannot give it,
you can take.
No heaven can come to us
     unless our hearts find rest in it today.
     Take heaven.
No peace lies in the future
     which is not hidden in this present little instant.
     Take peace.

*Source unknown.

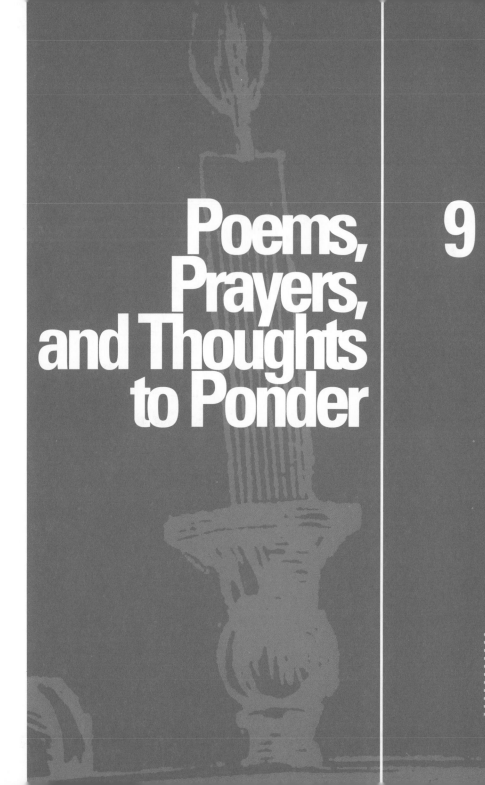

Poems, Prayers, and Thoughts to Ponder

9

Prayer for a Busy Day*

Dear God,

When the day is too busy and the voices too loud,

when there is too much on my mind and too little in my heart,

when I plan too much for tomorrow and explain too much about yesterday,

when faith is a Sunday word and "Let's be practical" my motto through the week,

when I have hidden my true feelings inside and then complained of being lonely and
misunderstood,

when I am quite hopelessly lost and don't even have sense enough to know it—

Be my good shepherd and my friend.

Gather up my jangled nerves, my tensed muscles, my anxious and fluttering heart.

Gather up my fearful heart and hold it warmly in your hand.

Send life pulsing through it like an irresistible flood.

Quicken me to a quivering blaze, excited and alive.

But show me how to be quiet, too.

Teach me to be still.

In deep stillness let me rest.

Let silence surround me like a friend, calming me and instructing me with deeper wisdom from
within.

When my day is too busy and the voices are all too loud,

be my good shepherd and my friend.

Amen.

*Used by permission of Rev. George L. Miller, D Min.

Prayer for Responsive Reading*

The lure and clamor of the world are so
      consuming, tumultuous, strident,
      and demanding.
   We scarcely hear your still, small,
      whispered voice of calm.
Quiet our restless nature as we breathe in
      deeply your peace and tranquility.
   Remove our fears, strivings, and
      self-centered goals.
Attune us to your spirit.
   Fill us with your divine presence.
Re-create us to embody your faith, love,
      peace, and joy.
   In the name of Jesus we pray.
Amen.

*Let mystery have its place in you; do not be always turning up your whole soil with the plowshare of self-examination, but leave a little fallow corner in your heart ready for any seed the winds may bring, and reserve a nook of shadow for the passing bird; keep a place in your heart for the unexpected guests, an altar for unknown God.

Emptiness and Availability*

Emptiness is a key word in describing the experience of acceptance. And again, I find confirmation in the work of Elisabeth Kubler-Ross, who says that the stage of acceptance in a dying person "should not be mistaken for a happy stage. It is almost void of feelings." Perhaps many of us have had that sense, when we have finally accepted a difficult reality and there is simply a hole inside us, not a raw place or a sinking space but a simple emptiness. So often it is in such moments that a larger power flows through our lives, through the space which has been emptied in us by acceptance.

I have had that experience in teaching when I struggle to plan a class, but work as I might nothing seems right; so I finally give up, yield to my own inability, walk into class feeling empty and unprepared—and in that state am somehow able to be an open conduit for truth to flow between me and my students. Those are the times the students say how good it was—not the times when I am filled with plans which do not yield to the power of the Spirit!

*May Iwahashi, "Prayer for Responsive Reading," *alive now!* Jul/Aug 1989, p. 49. Used by permission.

Amiel's Journal, translated by Mrs. Humphrey Ward (New York: A. L. Burt, Co., Publishers), as cited in *Daybook*, edited by Mary and Nancy Hiles, Summer 1991, p. 20.

*Parker J. Palmer, *The Promise of Paradox* (Washington, DC: The Servant Leadership Press, 1993).

Time Enough . . . .*

Often we're not as pressed for time as much as we *feel* we're pressed for time. I remember several years ago becoming so pressed by the demands of teaching at Yale that I took a prayer sabbatical to the Trappist monastery at Genesee, New York. No teaching, lecturing, or counseling—just solitude and prayer.

The second day there, a group of students from Genesee College walked in and asked, "Henri, can you give us a retreat?"

Of course at the monastery that was not my decision, but I said to the abbot, "I came here from the university to get away from that type of thing. These students have asked for five meditations, an enormous amount of work and preparation. I don't want to do it."

The abbot said, "You're going to do it."

"What do you mean? Why should I spend my sabbatical time preparing all those things?"

"Prepare?" he replied. "You've been a Christian for forty years and a priest for twenty, and a few high school students want to have a retreat. Why do you have to prepare? What those boys and girls want is to be a part of your life in God for a few days. If you pray half an hour in the morning, sing in our choir for an hour, and do your spiritual reading, you will have so much to say you could give ten retreats."

The question, you see, is not to prepare but to live in a state of ongoing preparedness so that, when someone who is drowning in the world comes into your world, you are ready to reach out and help. It may be at four o'clock, six o'clock, or nine o'clock. One time you call it preaching, the next time teaching, then counseling, or later administration. But let them be part of your life in God—that's ministering.

*Why, O Lord, is it so hard for me to keep my heart directed toward you? Why do the many little things I want to do, and the many people I know, keep crowding into my mind, even during the hours that I am totally free to be with you and you alone? Why does my mind wander off in so many directions, and why does my heart desire the things that lead me astray? Are you not enough for me? Do I keep doubting your love and care, your mercy and grace? Do I keep wondering, in the centre of my being, whether you will give me all I need if I just keep my eyes on you?

Please accept my distractions, my fatigue, my irritations, and my faithless wanderings. You know me more deeply and fully than I know myself. You love me with a greater love than I can love myself. You even offer me more than I can desire. Look at me, see me in all my misery and inner confusion, and let me sense your presence in the midst of my turmoil. All I can do is show myself to you. Yet, I am afraid to do so. I am afraid that you will reject me. But I know—with the knowledge of faith—that you desire to give me your love. The only thing you ask of me is not to hide from you, not run away in despair, not to act as if you were a relentless despot.

Take my tired body, my confused mind, and my restless soul into your arms and give me rest, simple quiet rest. Do I ask too much too soon? I should not worry about that. You will let me know. Come, Lord Jesus, come. Amen.

*From "Time Enough to Minister," by Henri J. M. Nouwen, as cited in *A Guide to Prayer for Ministers and Other Servants* (Nashville: The Upper Room, 1983), p. 124.

*From *A Cry for Mercy*, by Henri J. M. Nouwen, pp. 26–27. Copyright © 1981 by Henri J. M. Nouwen. Used by permission of Doubleday, a division of Bantam Doubleday Dell Publishing Group, Inc.

The Road Ahead*

My Lord God, I have no idea where I am going. I do not see the road ahead of me. I cannot know for certain where it will end. Nor do I really know myself, and the fact that I think I am following your will does not mean that I am actually doing so. But I believe that the desire to please you does in fact please you. And I hope I have that desire in all that I am doing. I hope that I will never do anything apart from that desire. And I know that if I do this you will lead me by the right road, though I may know nothing about it. Therefore I will trust you always though I may seem to be lost and in the shadow of death. I will not fear, for you are ever with me, and you will never leave me to face my perils alone.

Pieces of a Lifetime*

The Hebrew word for angel is *malech, w*hich also means messenger. One who is sent. . . .

There must have been a time when you entered a room and met someone and after a while you understood that unknown to either of you there was a reason you had met. You had changed the other or he had changed you. By some word or deed or just by your presence the errand had been completed. Then perhaps you were a little bewildered or humbled or grateful. And it was over.

Each lifetime is the pieces of a jigsaw puzzle.
For some there are more pieces.
For others the puzzle is more difficult to assemble.

Some seem to be born with a nearly completed puzzle.
And so it goes.
Souls going this way and that
Trying to assemble the myriad parts.

But know this. No one has within themselves
All the pieces to their puzzle.
Like before the days when they used to seal
jigsaw puzzles in cellophane. Ensuring that
All the pieces were there.

Everyone carries with them at least one and probably
Many pieces to someone else's puzzle.
Sometimes they know it.
Sometimes they don't.

And when you present your piece
Which is worthless to you,
To another, whether you know it or not,
Whether they know it or not,
You are a messenger from the Most High.

*"The Road Ahead," from *Thoughts in Solitude*, by Thomas Merton, p. 103. Copyright © 1956, 1958 by the Abbey of Our Lady of Gethsemani. Copyright renewed © 1986 by Trustees of the Merton Legacy Trust. Reprinted by permission of Farrar, Straus & Giroux, Inc.

*Excerpt from *Honey from the Rock: An Easy Introduction to Jewish Mysticism*, by Lawrence Kushner (Woodstock, VT: Jewish Lights Publishing, 1990). Order by mail or call (800) 962-4544. Permission granted by Jewish Lights Publishing, P. O. Box 237, Woodstock, VT 05091.

All hiding-places reveal God.
If you want to escape God,
 S/he runs into your lap.
For,
 God is at home.
 It is we who have gone out for a walk.*

*Reprinted with permission from *Meditations with Meister Eckhart*, by Matthew Fox, p. 15. Copyright © 1982 Bear & Co., Santa Fe, NM.

The eye with which I see God
 is the same eye with which God sees
 me.*

*Reprinted with permission from *Meditations with Meister Eckhart*, by Matthew Fox, p. 21. Copyright © 1982 Bear & Co., Santa Fe, NM.

O God, I am seeking
 for ways to be
less encumbered;
 ways to
simplify my life;
 ways to build
spaces and silences
 into a life full
 of busyness
 and noise.
Teach me to find that
 quiet center of self
 that you have
hidden within me,
 a resting in
 your presence.*

*Jamie L. Watkins, "An Opening Prayer," in *alive now!* Jul/Aug 1989, p. 31.

*If the heart wanders or is distracted, bring it back to the point quite gently and replace it tenderly in its Master's presence. And even if you did nothing during the whole of your hour but bring your heart back and place it again in Our Lord's presence, though it went away every time you brought it back, your hour would be very well employed.

*St. Francis de Sales, 1567–1622

A Prayer Before Silent Prayer*

Divine and Hidden Friend,
    I often feel that I fail at prayer,
    but I rejoice that your Spirit
    prays ceaselessly in the cellar of my
        heart.
Grant me the grace to sit still
    that I may hear the Spirit's silent song,
    ever flowing like a river deep within,
    singing my love for you.
Quiet my restless heart,
    calm my roving, runaway mind,
    as now, in communion with all the earth
    and her many-colored children,
    I enter into the song of love,
    the prayer of stillness.
Amen.

*Reprinted with permission from *Prayers for a Planetary Pilgrim*, by Edward Hays. Copyright 1988 Forest of Peace Publishing, Inc., 251 Muncie Rd., Leavenworth, KS 66048.

A Prayer for Departing*

Now it is time to continue on my road of life,
    and as I prepare to leave this holy
        place,
    may I fill the pockets of my heart
    with the memory of this prayerful
        remembrance.
So enriched, may I meet all that comes to me
    in a sacred and priestly way.

*Reprinted with permission from *Prayers for a Planetary Pilgrim*, by Edward Hays. Copyright 1988 Forest of Peace Publishing, Inc., 251 Muncie Rd., Leavenworth, KS 66048.

Words for the Divine

The following prayer was written using phrases for God which are found in Thomas Kelly's *A Testament of Devotion*. Kelly, a Quaker, spoke of God in words that provided a broader context for pondering the Holy One. Although his book, which was published in 1941, fails to use inclusive language, his references to the nature of God most certainly do.

There is a divine Abyss within us all, a holy Infinite Center, a Heart, a Life who speaks in us and through us to the world. We have all heard this holy Whisper at times. At times we have followed the Whisper, and amazing equilibrium of life, amazing effectiveness of living set in. But too many of us have heeded the Voice only at times. Only at times have we submitted to His holy guidance. We have not counted this Holy Thing within us to be the most precious thing in the world. We have not surrendered *all* else, to attend to it alone. Let me repeat. Most of us, I fear, have not surrendered all else, in order to attend to the Holy Within.*

Pray this prayer together, recognizing some of Kelly's phrases for God.

Divine Lover, take away our fear and convert our anxious, busy moments into opportunities to partake of your divine Whisper in new-found silence.
Loving Center, take away our selfishness, and convert our energies into healing and hopeful ministries to others.
Holy One, break in upon us and change us as we unlock closed doors and open to your love.
Light Within, take away our darkness and be a lamp for us, illuminating our way and the way of those we touch.
Center of Creation, be adored forever in our hearts and in our use of the many gifts we have been given.
Eternal Father, hear our prayer and welcome us home, now and when our time-now has become the *Eternal Now.*
Divine Presence, go with us now and in the days to come. Amen.**

*Thomas Kelly, *A Testament of Devotion*, p. 93. Copyright © 1941 by HarperCollins Publishers. Used by permission.

**Ann Z. Kulp, *A Testament of Devotion: Leader's Guide* (New York: HarperCollins Publishers, 1993), p. 43. Used by permission.

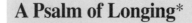

*Dear God,

Speak gently in my silence.
When the loud outer noises of my surroundings
and the loud inner noises of my fears
keep pulling me away from you,
help me to trust that you are still there.
Give me ears to listen to your small, soft voice saying,
"and I will give you rest . . .
For I am gentle and humble of heart."
Let that loving voice be my guide.

Amen.

Question: Why do I avoid silence?

A Psalm of Longing*

My spirit hungers for your love,
    O Divine Maker of hearts,
    for the taste of your joy
    and the aroma of your peace.

May this time of prayer
    fill me with the whisper of your presence
    and let me feel the touch
    of your hand upon my heart.

How I long for the depths of your love,
    to know your quiet constancy,
    the feast of your friendship
    that feeds me without end.

Oh, how my soul longs for you.
You elude all names we give you
    and dwell beyond the grasp of brilliant minds.
Your essence pulses within every atom
    yet extends beyond the far frontiers of space,
    unscanned by the strongest telescopes.
Awaken me to your presence,
    now this moment,
    in my heart.

*Excerpted from *With Open Hands*, by Henri J. M. Nouwen.
Copyright 1995 by Ave Maria Press, Notre Dame, IN 46556.

*Reprinted with permission from *Prayers for a Planetary Pilgrim*, by Edward
    Hays, p. 172. Copyright 1988 Forest Peace Publishing, Inc., 251 Muncie Rd.,
    Leavenworth, KS 66048.

Reflections on
The Wisdom of the Heart

Balance, discipline, illumination—these are the key words of wholeness, or holiness, for the words mean the same thing. It is not essentially new, but it needs to be rediscovered by each and every one individually.[*]

These key words . . . what do they mean? They probably mean something a little different to each of us, but I offer these thoughts for your reflection.

Balance
The state of equilibrium between "being" and "doing"; the "I am who I am" versus the "I am called to do and to act." Rarely are we *in* balance (even if we happen to be born under the zodiacal sign of Libra). For as a good friend once said, "You are continually seeking that balance." That seems to be one of the challenges of living.

Discipline
The commitments that we are willing to make in order to achieve our goals, whether they be spiritual, physical, mental, or social. Without some measure of discipline we are likely to succumb to the easiest, or most pressing, alternative—which more than likely will *not* be in sync with our heart's desire. These commitments may be to a time, or a place, or a habit. Whatever form they take, it is important to remember that excessive adherence to any pattern becomes addiction, which may be as unhealthy as no discipline at all! If we are honest, we are all addicted to some particular patterns of behavior that we depend on instead of God, leaving us constantly in need of God's grace. Spiritual disciplines, then, should not become so fixed that we cannot be open to new ways of experiencing God's presence, or perhaps—for a spell—no method at all. As Meister Eckhart said, "God is at home. It is we who have gone out for a walk."

Illumination
That stage of insight or awareness that tells us we are in God's presence; we are standing on holy ground. It might come through an experience, a reading, an observation, or a moment of silence. We may not even be sure what it is at that instant, only in recollection. We may have ambivalent feelings: wanting to run toward and away from the moment, unsure, half resisting, half eager. So it becomes extremely important that we exercise discernment, being willing to ask ourselves—unashamedly—questions about our experiences and feelings, our motives and desires. It is also important that we remember to give thanks for that hallowed moment, or perhaps for our uncertainty and bewilderment. Our faith is not built on an experience or a feeling, but in trust that God is faithful to hear us and be with us . . . no matter what happens.

To rediscover these three words means to keep reminding ourselves that God is continually being revealed to us, that we are most conscious of that presence when we are open, listening, and attentive to God's word and God's creation.

[*]Henry Miller, *The Wisdom of the Heart* (New York: New Directions, 1941), as cited in *Daybook*, May 22–June 18, 1989, p. 9.

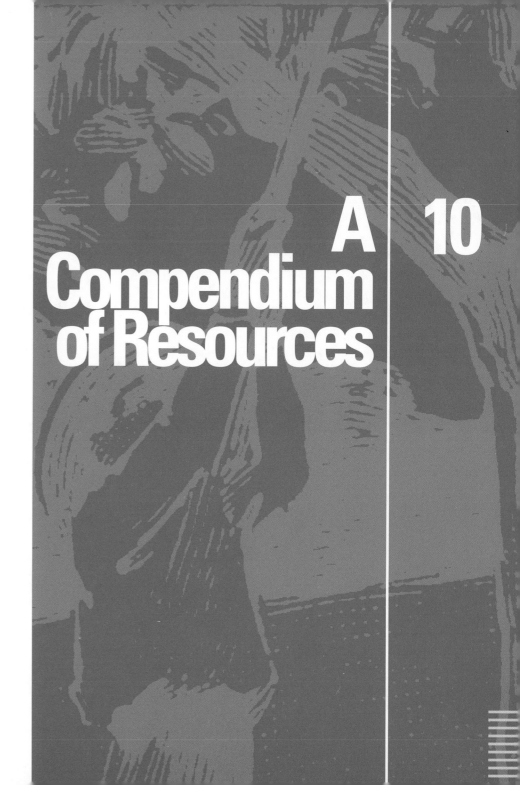

A Compendium of Resources

A 10

The Body as a Spiritual Vessel

Campbell, Peter A. and Edwin M. McMahon. *BioSpirituality: Focusing as a Way to Grow*. Chicago: Loyola University Press, 1985. The method of focusing as developed by Eugene Gendlin of the University of Chicago has shifted from a therapy to a form of spiritual meditation. The authors believe that attention to the body's wisdom is needed today for Christian spirituality. They want to reunite the head (thinking and processing) with the body, thus attending to meaning that is felt in the body.

Roth, Nancy. *A New Christian Yoga*. Boston: Cowley Press, 1989. This thin, notebook-sized handbook uses full-page illustrations to describe basic yoga postures. An opening section speaks of our bodies as incarnational, as the temple of the Holy Spirit. The attitude that is presented is that of wholeness through body prayer. Christian words are substituted for some of the more traditional Eastern terms. It offers additional suggestions for use in simple relaxation.

Wuellner, Flora Slosson. *Prayer and Our Bodies*. Nashville: Upper Room, 1987. A book that calls for us to observe part of God's creation—our bodies—and to honor, pray with (not just for), and develop a new relationship with our bodies. Includes some practices and meditations.

Contemporary Versions of the Psalms

Chamberlain, Gary. *The Psalms: A New Translation for Prayer and Worship*. Nashville: Upper Room, 1984. Working from the original Hebrew texts, the author aims to understand the psalm as a whole. Inclusive language used.

Mitchell, Stephen. *A Book of Psalms: Selected and Adapted from the Hebrew*. New York: HarperCollins, 1994. The author, noted for his translations of Job and the Tao Te Ching, has selected fifty of the greatest psalms from the Hebrew Bible. He is noted for his scholarly work and in this version has recreated the dense supple music of Hebrew verse.

Darkness of Soul

DelBene, Ron. *Into the Light: A Simple Way to Pray with the Sick and the Dying*. Nashville: Upper Room, 1988. Practical suggestions for when we often feel hopeless and powerless.

Green, Thomas H. *When the Well Runs Dry: Prayer Beyond the Beginnings*. Notre Dame, IN: Ave Maria Press, 1979. For those experiencing the "dark night of the soul," this book offers solace and encouragement to see the situation as an opportunity for growth.

Rupp, Joyce. *Little Pieces of Light: Darkness and Personal Growth*. Mahwah, NJ: Paulist, 1994. A small book of encouragement, urging readers to learn to abide in the womb of nurturing during dark times.

Rupp, Joyce. *Praying Our Goodbyes*. Notre Dame, IN: Ave Maria Press, 1988. A book for anyone who has experienced loss, whether it be a job, the end of a relationship, the death of a loved one, a financial struggle, a midlife crisis, or an extended illness. It includes probing questions and twenty-four prayer experiences.

St. John of the Cross. *Dark Night of the Soul,* translated and edited by E. Allison Peers. New York: Image, 1959. A Spanish mystic of the sixteenth century, a soulmate of St. Teresa of Avila, writes about difficult experiences associated with dry periods in the spiritual life.

▌ Devotions and Inspiration

Chamberlain, Gary. *The Psalms: A New Translation for Prayer and Worship*. Nashville: Upper Room, 1984. Working from the original Hebrew texts, the author aims to understand the psalm as a whole. Inclusive language is used throughout.

Edelman, Marian Wright. *Guide My Feet: Prayers and Meditations on Loving and Working for Children*. Boston: Beacon Press, 1995. A collection of familiar and original prayers and poems that relate to children and our relationship to them for the sake of the world's future.

Hays, Edward. *Prayers for a Planetary Pilgrim: A Personal Manual for Prayer and Ritual*. Easton, KS: Forest of Peace Books, 1988. A welcome collection of contemporary prayers and forms suitable for group or individual use. (See "A Prayer Before Silent Prayer," page 150.)

Jäger, Willis. *Contemplation: A Christian Path*. Liguori, MO: Triumph, 1994. A sourcebook on the subject that surveys the kinds of approaches that appeal to different personalities. It uses psychological insights as well as references to the mystics such as Meister Eckhart and St. John of the Cross. The book deals with the issues one faces when choosing such a path.

Job, Reuben P. and Norman Shawchuck. *A Guide to Prayer for All God's People*. Nashville: Upper Room, 1990. Weekly devotional themes with Scripture readings for each day, prayers, selected readings from spiritual classics, and a chosen hymn.

Job, Reuben P. and Norman Shawchuck. *A Guide to Prayer for Ministers and Other Servants*. Nashville: Upper Room, 1983. Weekly devotional themes with Scripture readings for each day, prayers, selected readings from spiritual classics, and a chosen hymn. Also twelve retreat models. Popular handbook with both clergy and laity.

Loder, Ted. *Guerrillas of Grace*. San Diego, CA: LuraMedia, 1984. A book of free-verse prayers that speak to our needs, hopes, and failures. Widely used by clergy and laity.

Marty, Martin and Micah Marty. *Our Hope for Years to Come: The Search for Spiritual Sanctuary*. Minneapolis: Augsburg Fortress, 1995. Designed to go from Ash Wednesday to Easter (forty-seven days), this book can be used anytime, with its magnificent photographs of sanctuary spaces that are matched with a hymn verse, a brief reflection, and a Scripture notation. Each page has a theme to unite the whole. A book to lift the spirit and to treasure.

Merton, Thomas. *Thoughts in Solitude*. New York: Farrar, Straus, & Giroux, 1976. This book, now reprinted, is a timeless gem.

Nouwen, Henri J. M. *A Cry for Mercy: Prayers from the Genesee*. New York: Bantam Doubleday Dell, 1981. This book is the result of Nouwen's self-imposed discipline while at the Trappist monastery in New York's Genesee Valley. The prayers are very real and honest, and easily translated into models for personal or corporate use.

Roberts, Elizabeth and Elias Amidon. *Earth Prayers from Around the World*. San Francisco: HarperCollins, 1991. A collection of 365 prayers, poems, and invocations for honoring the earth. Selections are authored by a wide variety of sources such as Julian of Norwich, Dylan Thomas, Walt Whitman, Rumi, Wendell Berry, Native Americans, and Rabbi Abraham Heschel.

Schaffran, Janet and Pat Kozak. *More Than Words: Prayer and Ritual for Inclusive Communities*. Oak Park, IL: Meyer, Stone & Co., 1988. An assortment of prayers, songs, and formats to represent a wide variety of themes. Also includes four pages on images of God, a section on symbols and rituals, and another on inclusive language. An exceptional resource.

Weems, Ann. *Searching for Shalom: Resources for Creative Worship*. Louisville, KY: Westminster/John Knox Press, 1991. A collection of poignant poetry, stories, and dramas, and a few creative worship services.

Wiederkehr, Macrina. *Seasons of Your Heart: Prayers and Reflections*. San Francisco: HarperCollins, 1979; reprint, 1991. With simplicity and easy conversational style, Wiederkehr addresses God. She introduces fresh images and draws upon Scripture to pen a brief commentary on everyday life. Her life is truly lived out of her prayer, which she graciously shares with the reader.

Zundel, Veronica, ed. *Christian Classics: A Treasury of Christian Writings throughout the Centuries*. Copyright 1983 by Lion Publishing. Grand Rapids: Wm. B. Eerdmans Publishing Co., 1985. An anthology of specially selected writings from early Christian times through the twentieth century. Includes writings from the *Didache*, Origen, Augustine, the medieval mystics, Martin Luther, St. John of the Cross, George Herbert, Brother Lawrence, and Sören Kierkegaard. Concludes with Alexander Solzhenitsyn, Madeleine L'Engle, and Martin Luther King, Jr.

Zundel, Veronica, ed. *Eerdman's Book of Famous Prayers: A Treasury of Christian Prayers through the Centuries*. Copyright © 1983 by Lion Publishing. Grand Rapids:

Wm. B. Eerdmans Publishing Co., 1984. A beautiful and inclusive collection of prayers from the Bible, Celts, Medieval Mystics, and subsequent notables throughout the world. Includes prayers from Lorenzo Hammarskjöld, Dietrich Bonhoeffer, Mother Teresa, Thomas Merton, Martin Quoist, Henri J. M. Nouwen, and the Taizé Community.

▌ Digging Deeper — More Challenging Works

Edwards, Tilden. *Living in the Presence: Disciplines for the Spiritual Heart*. San Francisco: HarperSanFrancisco, 1987. For those who wish to delve deeper into prayer practices and understand more of the background information, this is a first rate selection. There are also suggestions for using these practices with groups, as well as twenty-seven exercises listed separately in each chapter. These exercises range from the use of the breath, praying with Scripture, the use of icons, and sound and silence.

Fox, Matthew. *The Coming of the Cosmic Christ*. San Francisco: HarperSanFrancisco, 1988. This book appears to be revolutionary in nature yet is grounded in the traditions of mysticism and an understanding of Jesus beyond history. Challenging, bold, provocative, and captivating.

Jäger, Willis. *Search for the Meaning of Life: Essays and Reflections on the Mystical Experience*. Liguori, MO: Triumph Books, 1995. This is a collection of lectures on the mystic path, both Christian and Eastern in nature. It is scholarly in nature, yet full of the kind of wisdom that entices and convinces.

Johnson, Ben Campbell. *Discerning God's Will*. Louisville, KY: Westminster/John Knox Press, 1990. The author writes about the human quest to find one's purpose in life and shows that the search for meaning is synonymous with the quest for the will of God. Reflection exercises along with a brief guide to the process of discernment are included.

Kelsey, Morton T. *The Other Side of Silence: A Guide to Christian Meditation*. Ramsey, NJ: Paulist Press, 1976. A practical manual that covers the basic issues of meditation, offers help in preparation, and discusses the use of silence, images, and the inner world. The last section is a collection of guided images, as well as samples of work with dreams and the imagination.

Kushner, Lawrence. *Honey from the Rock: An Easy Introduction to Jewish Mysticism*. Woodstock, VT: Jewish Lights, 1990. A book that engages the mind and imagination, at times seeming to connect with modern science, then quickly sending the reader off to angelic realms. Full of selections for meditation as well as discussion.

May, Gerald G. *Simply Sane: The Spirituality of Mental Health*. New York: Crossroad, 1993. The subtitle in the original edition was *"Stop Fixing Yourself and Start Really Living,"* which seems to describe the author's primary intent. Still, the later version treats us to the author's updated personal comments and backward look, adding fresh insights on trust, solitude, and prayer.

May, Gerald G. *Will and Spirit: A Contemplative Psychology*. San Francisco: HarperSanFrancisco, 1987. A profound tome on the human's search for understanding about love, energy, evil, willingness even while experiencing willfulness, and the many facets of spiritual awareness.

Myss, Caroline. *Anatomy of the Spirit: The Seven Stages of Power and Healing*. New York: Random House, 1996. This book is included because it opens us to a new frontier in the mind-body-spirit connection by dealing with the field of intuition, a kind of spiritual insight. The author points out the connectedness between the Hindu chakras, the Christian sacraments, and the Jewish Kabbalah Tree of Life. It also offers the reader information on developing one's own sense of awareness.

Tuoti, Frank X. *Why Not Be a Mystic? An Irresistible Invitation to Experience the Presence of God— Here and Now*. New York: Crossroad, 1995. Written by a Trappist monk who lived and studied with Thomas Merton, this book addresses the treasure to be found in seeking God through contemplation. It enlightens with rich references and lightens with humor and story.

▌ Dreams as a Spiritual Tool

Kelsey, Morton T. *Dreams: A Way to Listen to God*. New York: Paulist Press, 1978. The author shows us how to pay attention to the inner images and voices emerging from the depths of our beings. He relates this to our relationship with God.

Kelsey, Morton T. *God, Dreams, and Revelation: A Christian Interpretation of Dreams*. Minneapolis: Augsburg Fortress, 1968; reprint, 1974. The author traces the development of Judeo-Christian attitudes about dreams from Old and New Testament times to the present. Practical suggestions are offered for use of this potential resource hidden within.

Sanford, John A. *Dreams: God's Forgotten Language*. San Francisco: HarperSanFrancisco, 1989. Examples from real life are matched with scriptural references in this book. Other sections explore biblical dreams and visions and delve into Jungian psychology, archetypal figures, and the role of opposites. Sanford seeks to understand the language of the soul; he believes that our dreams are in the service of our wholeness.

Savary, Louis, P. Berne, and S. K. Williams. *Dreams and Spiritual Growth: A Christian Approach to Dreamwork*. Ramsey, NJ: Paulist Press, 1984. An experienced team presents their understanding of the connection and usefulness of dreams as related to the spiritual life.

▌ Historical Perspectives

Bouyer, Louis, ed. *A History of Christian Spirituality*. Vol. 3: *Orthodox Spirituality and Protestant and Anglican Spirituality*. San Francisco: Seabury/HarperCollins, 1969. Part of a series that examines tradition and practice through the ages. A 1994 version is available through distributors at (718) 261-1704.

Holmes, Urban T. *A History of Christian Spirituality*. San Francisco: Seabury/HarperCollins, 1980. Both a text and a source of information for the average layperson, this manageable book covers the subject of prayer and its history from the early church to the present. The table of contents itself is a valuable outline of spiritual schools and individuals. Though not listed in *Books in Print*, it is frequently found on library shelves.

Rice, Howard L. *Reformed Spirituality: An Introduction for Believers*. Louisville, KY: Westminster/John Knox Press, 1991. While covering many of the topics standard to the spiritual life, as well as the more recent reclaimed practice of spiritual direction, the author frames all within the context of Reformed Christianity. This is not to mean limited in nature, but more expansive, as the reader is led through a wealth of material previously overlooked or ignored. It can guide any Christian to a more holistic understanding of spirituality.

▌ IONA Community Materials

The tapes and music books of the Wild Goose Worship Group are available from G.I.A. Publications, Inc., 7404 South Mason Ave., Chicago, IL 60638.

▌A Jungian Approach to the Spiritual Life

Caprio, Betsy. *The Woman Sealed in the Tower: A Psychological Approach to Feminine Spirituality*. Ramsey, NJ: Paulist Press, 1982. Using the legend of Saint Barbara, which developed into *Rapunzel,* the author explores the masculine and feminine principles as well as the symbolic elements of earth, air, fire, and water. Exercises are provided for personal enlightenment.

Caprio, Betsy and Thomas M. Hedberg. *Coming Home: A Handbook for Exploring the Sanctuary Within*. Mahwah, NJ: Paulist Press, 1986. Drawing on the insights of Carl Jung, the authors explore the urge to "come home." This is discerned as an inner place, a promised land of its own. The book provides an abundant source of paths from which to choose our journey. It is accompanied by interesting sketches and stories. A leader's guide is also available.

Houston, Jean. *The Search for the Beloved: Journeys in Mythology and Sacred Psychology*. Copyright 1987 by Jean Houston. Los Angeles: Jeremy P. Tarcher, Inc. 1987. A guidebook into the realm of human experience and longing, this search leads one to explore new language, challenging ideas, ancient myths, and sacred meanings from the stories.

Jung, Carl G. *Man and His Symbols*. Garden City, NY: Doubleday, 1964. This work bears seeing, if not reading, in order to behold the collection of art within. The importance of dreams, symbols, the shadow, and the masculine/feminine counterparts is demonstrated through word and picture. A background book found in most libraries. (See also books by Morton Kelsey and John A. Sanford on page 157.)

▌Periodicals

alive now! edited by George R. Graham. Published bimonthly by The Upper Room, Nashville, TN 37202 (800) 925-6847. A collection of contemporary thought on a variety of themes. Integrates photographs, poetry, prose, Scripture, and questions for reflection or discussion.

Daybook, edited by Marv and Nancy Hiles. Published quarterly by Iona Center, Inc., 1084 Cedar Lane, Cloverdale, CA 95425 (707) 894–2728. This is a non-profit organization dedicated to the nurture of spiritual life through publications, retreats, programs, and lectures. A selection of prose or poetry is given for each day and a breath prayer for the week. Authors may or may not be familiar; the quotations provide much food for thought and meditation. The editor writes a cover article around a quarterly theme.

OSMT Journal, Washington, DC. The Order of Saints Martin and Teresa is a family of individuals and communities committed to following Christ by observing spiritual disciplines and working for reconciliation through nonviolent peacemaking. Of Lutheran origin, but ecumenical. Write to *OSMT Journal,* 1861 Newton St. N.W., Washington, DC 20010.

Weavings, edited by John S. Mogabgab. Published bimonthly by The Upper Room, Nashville, TN 37202 (800) 925-6847. Articles by a wide variety of authors on a specific theme each issue. Includes several book reviews and appealing art design.

▌ Prayer Practices and Simple Meditation

Adam, David. *The Edge of Glory: Prayers in the Celtic Tradition*. Harrisburg, PA: Morehouse Publishing Co., 1988. An attractive little collection of prayers—traditional and ancient—for personal or group use.

Bloom, Anthony. *Beginning to Pray*. Ramsey, NJ: Paulist Press, 1982. A delightful modern spiritual classic by an Orthodox archbishop for people at all levels of spiritual development.

Bohler, Carolyn Stahl. *Opening to God: Guided Imagery Meditation on Scripture*. Nashville: Upper Room, 1996. Fifty different Scriptures are given with a format for usage. Excellent guidance for each session. Completely revised and expanded.

Borysenko, Joan. *Pocketful of Miracles: Prayers, Meditations, and Affirmations to Nurture Your Spirit Every Day of the Year*. New York: Warner, 1994. A small pocketbook with a page for each day that offers a "Seed Thought" and a "Prayer/Practice." While it draws from all traditions, it gives fresh perspectives to Christian Scripture and understanding. A delightful friend to carry with you.

Brooke, Avery. *Learning and Teaching Christian Meditation*. Nashville: Upper Room, 1990. An introductory book on meditation, that is, "listening prayer," with suggestions for group or individual practice along with application to Scripture.

Broyles, Ann. *Journaling—A Spirit Journey*. Nashville: Upper Room, 1988. An excellent introduction to prayer patterns with space for reflection through "journaling."

Chaffee, Paul. *Spirit Awakening: A Book of Practices*. San Francisco: Word Press, 1988. An excellent book on meditation with background on the Reformed tradition, along with suggested experiences.

DelBene, Ron, with Mary and Herb Montgomery. *The Breath of Life: A Simple Way to Pray*. Nashville: Upper Room, 1992. A whole book devoted to the practice of the breath prayer—a short prayer that helps one to become still, aware, and open to God's presence.

de Mello, Anthony. *Sadhana—A Way to God: Christian Exercises in Eastern Form*. New York: Image, 1984. Although listed as Eastern, most of these practices are now well-accepted in Christian circles. This is one of the best handbooks for

exploring spiritual disciplines individually or as a group. Explanations, stories, and a variety of practices to choose from.

de Mello, Anthony. *Wellsprings: A Book of Spiritual Exercises*. Garden City, NY: Doubleday, 1984. Through the use of guided imagery on assorted themes, de Mello leads readers (or listeners) into personal journeys of the spirit.

Hays, Edward M. *Prayers for a Planetary Pilgrim: A Personal Manual for Prayer and Ritual*. Leavenworth, KS: Forest of Peace, 1989. Virtually a handbook of prayers for all occasions, designed to offer selections by season, time of day, and occasion. Includes the psalms, as well as exercises and instructions for personal study. Extremely valuable resource.

Jäger, Willis. *Contemplation: A Christian Path*. Liguori, MO: Triumph, 1994. A sourcebook that surveys the kinds of approaches that appeal to different personalities. It uses psychological insights, as well as references to mystics such as Meister Eckhart and St. John of the Cross. The book deals with the issues one faces when choosing such a path.

Johnson, Ben Campbell. *To Pray God's Will*. Louisville, KY: Westminster/John Knox Press, 1987. Looking upon Christian life as a spiritual journey, the author discusses the importance of prayer, the inevitable desert, and spiritual companionship. Includes chapter exercises for individuals or groups. There is also an excellent summary on how to "journal" in the appendix.

Kelly, Marcia and Jack. *One Hundred Graces*. New York: Bell Tower, 1992. A book filled with inspiring words from interesting sources, plus artistic calligraphic renditions and a bookmark ribbon. Also an excellent gift book.

Killinger, John. *Beginning Prayer*. Nashville: Upper Room, 1993. Not necessarily for beginners, but for those who are interested in looking at a variety of ways to approach prayer. The introduction addresses times, places, postures, moods, and attitudes. The methods include silence, the Jesus Prayer, meditating on Scripture, memories, dreams, imaging, and "journaling."

Meehan, Bridget Mary. *Exploring the Feminine Face of God*. Kansas City, MO: Sheed & Ward, 1991. This book, for both men and women, introduces the reader to various feminine images of God. These images are presented through Scripture, the Christian mystics, and contemporary worship.

Merton, Thomas. *New Seeds of Contemplation*. New York: New Directions, 1972. A collection of personal vignettes, meditations, and insights from this famous contemplative that remain ever relevant.

Moremen, Bill. *Watch and Pray*. St. Louis: United Church Resources. A six-session booklet using the SHALEM model: focusing on sounds and silence, sensations and relaxation, and breath and spirit.

Morgan, Henry, ed. *Approaches to Prayer: A Resource Book for Groups and Individuals*. Harrisburg, PA: Morehouse Publishing Co., 1993. This book provides tools for groups and individuals in worship and exploration, as a result of a group experiment based in South London, England. The foreword is by Alan Jones of Grace Cathedral, San Francisco. He notes that the authors are aware that religion is an affair of the imagination before it is a matter of formulas and dogmas. The layout is both appealing and filled with ideas.

Nhat Hanh, Thich. *The Miracle of Mindfulness: A Manual on Meditation*. Boston: Beacon Press, 1976. An introduction to meditation, a famous story by Tolstoy, and thirty-two exercises to help one relax into a more contemplative state. Learn how to appreciate the cup in your hands, the washing of dishes, and simple acts that we take for granted.

Nouwen, Henri J. M. *Behold the Beauty of the Lord: Praying with Icons*. Notre Dame, IN: Ave Maria Press, 1987. An exceptional introduction to the meaning and use of icons in a small book that includes four of the best in fold-out form: The Holy Trinity, the Virgin of Vladimir, the Savior of Zvenigorod, and the Descent of the Holy Spirit. To Nouwen these icons represent four aspects of the salvation mystery: dwelling in the house of love, truly belonging to God, coming face to face with the Lord, and being commissioned to liberate the world—and together express our origin and destiny. If using these icons is unfamiliar, the author's commentary and simple directions should remove any apprehensions.

Nouwen, Henri J. M. *With Open Hands* (illus.). Notre Dame, IN: Ave Maria Press, 1995. Filled with moving photographs, this book is one of Nouwen's early writings on prayer. He begins with "clenched fists" and concludes with "open hands," moving through silence, acceptance, hope, compassion, and revolution.

Progoff, Ira. *The Well and the Cathedral: An Entrance Meditation*. New York: Dialogue House Library, 1983. One of several volumes that can be used alone or with groups. There is a journal page opposite each segment. The guided imagery can be used as a whole or divided into the marked sections, such as "Muddy/Clear: The Mirror of the Water" and "The Downward/Upward Journey."

Roth, Nancy. *Organic Prayer: Cultivating Your Relationship with God* (illus.). Boston: Cowley Press, 1993. A remarkably inviting book that parallels prayer life with the garden. The reader is encouraged to make use of all senses, to see, taste, touch, hear, smell, focus, walk. There is some "spadework" in each two-page chapter, together with questions and a guided practice. Titles are built around soil, seeds, water, compost, pests, and harvest, and end with Easter!

Rupp, Joyce. *May I Have This Dance?* Notre Dame, IN: Ave Maria Press, 1992. An invitation to join with God in the dance of life through monthly themes. Each section explores a theme and is followed by prayer suggestions that include litanies, creative writing, guided meditations, and ideas for reflection and journal writing.

Rupp, Joyce. *The Star in My Heart: Experiencing Sophia, Inner Wisdom*. San Diego: LuraMedia, 1990. A pastor says, "A treasure-house of wisdom for all who value the inner life, and a sensitive and practical guide for inner exploration." Experiencing the feminine part of ourselves (male or female) and the Divine.

Steere, Douglas. *Dimensions of Prayer: Cultivating a Relationship with God*. Nashville: Upper Room, 1997. A new edition of an easy-to-read classic by a noted Quaker that holds appeal for both novice and experienced prayer. It includes biblical references, as well as devotional suggestions.

Steindl-Rast, Brother David. *Gratefulness, the Heart of Prayer: An Approach to Life in Fullness*. Ramsey, NJ: Paulist Press, 1984. A book that will be read and reread. A simple message that helps one come to terms with the act of gratitude in prayer.

Ulanov, Ann and Barry. *Primary Speech: A Psychology of Prayer*. Atlanta: John Knox Press, 1982. The language, images, and approach in this book make one look forward to discovering the naturalness of prayer.

Ward, Elaine M. *Encountering God*. Brea, CA: Educational Ministries, 1990. A six-session series using stories, exercises, and discussion as God is encountered through silence, service, dreams, imagination, story, Scripture, love, and creation.

Weatherhead, Leslie D. *The Will of God*. Nashville: Abingdon Press, 1972. A timeless book on a subject that causes much discussion and speculation. A truly helpful approach for those wrestling with the cause of pain and suffering. Three different aspects of God's will are given with examples.

▌ Praying/Meditating with Scripture

Bonhoeffer, Dietrich. *Meditating on the Word* (large print). New York: Walker & Co., 1988. Includes his instructions for meditations, as well as sermons and meditations on the psalms.

Canham, Elizabeth. *Praying the Bible*. Boston: Cowley Press, 1987. With insight and occasional humor, the author presents practical forms for using biblical words. Scattered throughout are select pieces of literature that lift and guide. It is a book that seems to have been truly lived out by the author.

Cooper, Joan. *Guided Meditation and the Teaching of Jesus*. Rockport, MA: Element Books, 1990. Guided meditation sections are on growth, the journey, the seed, the power of Jesus, and the substance of life. They use methods that the author believes Jesus used in teaching.

Douglas-Klotz, Neil, trans. *Prayers of the Cosmos: Meditations on the Aramaic Words of Jesus*. San Francisco: HarperSanFrancisco, 1993. The Lord's Prayer, the Beatitudes, and other sayings of Jesus are translated and accompanied by commentary. Suggestions are also given for body prayers, ways to experience the words deep within.

Hall, Thelma. *Too Deep for Words: Rediscovering* Lectio Divina (with 500 Scripture Texts for Prayer). Mahwah, NJ: Paulist Press, 1988. An excellent tool for this method, as well as an outstanding collection of topical texts for any use.

Keating, Thomas. *Open Mind, Open Heart: The Contemplative Dimension of the Gospel*. New York: Continuum, 1995. Considered "the bible of centering prayer" by many people. A thorough review of contemplative practice with excellent appendixes and summaries.

Smith, Martin. *The Word is Very Near You: A Guide to Praying with Scripture*. Boston: Cowley Press, 1989. This volume with hundreds of scriptural passages is organized by theme. There are also introductory chapters stressing the importance of pausing to converse with God, being touched by Scripture, and actually entering into the story.

Wiederkehr, Macrina. *A Tree Full of Angels: Seeing the Holy in the Ordinary*. New York: Harper & Row, 1988. Many chapters in this book are devoted to a superior rendering of *Lectio Divina* (Divine Reading). It is usable, anecdotal, and delightful.

▌ Recommended Music: Cassettes and Compact Discs

These selections are based on their use at retreats, workshops, or the Shalem Institute's course that I lead called "Music as a Doorway to Prayer." Codes are either by recording house, ISBN, or the number under the bar code on the back of the compact disc (BC).

Chant

Chant for Christmas—Choralschola der Wiener Hofburgkapelle. Chants of hymns and vespers for Christmastide that can be used at any time. (Philips 416808-2) (BC: 28941-68082)

A Feather on the Breath of God: Sequences and Hymns by Abbess Hildegard of Bingen. A more traditional version of the medieval chant that she composed. (BC: 34571-16039)

O Great Spirit. A chant by "On Wings of Song" singers, produced by Robert Gass. Quite lovely. Spring Hill Music, P.O. Box 800, Boulder, CO 80306. (SHM-1009)

Officium—Jan Garbarek, saxophonist, and The Hilliard Ensemble. This is a captivating rendition of early forms of music that suggest chant, polyphony, and Renaissance motets. The soprano and tenor sax adds a haunting touch to the voices that experiment with the wide variety of approaches to human sound from preliterate to Dufay and the Morales piece from the Officium defunctorum. With booklet and words. (ECM 1525) (BC: 81182–15252)

Sound Faith. Chants used at the Shalem Institute for Spiritual Formation. An actual group singing the chants with the leader Isabella Bates in the Chapel of Joseph of Arimathea, Washington National Cathedral. She sings the chant once, then the group sings it five times. Easy to learn by joining in at the beginning, fading it out, then moving on at one's own rhythm. (To order, contact Isabella Bates, 2303 Chain Bridge Road, N.W., Washington, DC 20016.)

Vision: The Music of Hildegard von Bingen. A modern rendition of the medieval music, occasionally blending the original chant with synthesizers. Booklet with words. Also has a companion book (see "Spiritual Classics" on pages 168–169). (S21-18449) (BC: 24381-84492)

Contemporary Arrangements

Celtic Mass for the Sea. This contemporary mass celebrates the reverence of ancient peoples for the sea's majesty, ferocity, and vitality. It is a modern form that celebrates nature and uses pre-Christian as well as Christian writings that were well researched. Irish instruments. Commissioned by the Canadian Broadcasting Co. (ERAD 149) (BC: 74718-11492)

Circlesongs—Bobby McFerrin. A *most* unusual approach to music, McFerrin improvises "on the spot" with his group of twelve singers. These songs are without words, a spontaneous form of sacred music that dates back centuries where tribal gatherings would respond to the opening sound or phrase. McFerrin believes that "one of the simplest and most direct ways of praying and meditating is through singing, and singing in community is exceptionally powerful." With interesting descriptive booklet. (SK 62734) (BC: 7464–62734–2)

Missa Gaia/Earth Mass—Paul Winter. A mass in celebration of Mother Earth recorded live in the Cathedral of St. John the Divine and the Grand Canyon. A spectacular listening adventure. Living Music. (CD #LD0002) (BC: 10488-00022)

Passion—Peter Gabriel. This is the music written for the movie "The Last Temptation of Christ." Contains Middle-Eastern rhythms and tones, as well as those that are sensuous and sublime. The particular selections for meditation are "With This Love" (both the instrumental and choral) and "Bread and Wine." (Geffen: 24206-2) (BC: 21585-07042)

Rosa Mystica—Therese Schroeder-Sheker. This is an album using harp, voice, psalteries, and bells. It uses medieval music and the rose mystery that so moved Rilke, Rumi, and T.S. Eliot. Celestial Harmonies. (LC7869) (BC: 13711-30342)

Guided Imagery

Go in Peace. A meditation tape with music. Words by Marjorie Bankson. (LAM-206) LuraMedia, P.O. Box 261668, San Diego, CA 92126 (619) 578-1948.

Hymns or Sacred Choral Music

Agnus Dei: Music for Inner Harmony—
The Choir of New College, Oxford.
An exceedingly professional
recording of twelve classical sacred
pieces, including Mendelssohn's
"Hear My Prayer"; Elgar's "Lux
aeterna"; Rachmaninoff's "Ave
Maria"; Barber's "Agnus Dei"; and
Bach's "Jesu, Joy of Man's
Desiring." Exquisite. (Erato
0630–14634–2)

*Allegri: Miserere/Palestrina: Stabat
Mater—*Choir of King's College,
Cambridge. The "Miserere" was
sung each year in the Sistine Chapel
during Holy Week from the mid-
seventeenth century until 1870. It
was one of the choir's most
jealously guarded treasures, yet
Mozart at age 14 visited Rome and
achieved the notable feat of writing
the work out from memory after a
single hearing. An incredibly
sublime work. Also sung in English
by the Choir of Trinity College,
Cambridge, on the *Voce* disk below.
(CD 421 147-2)

*Ave Maria—*Kiri te Kanawa and the
Choir of St. Paul's Cathedral.
Features "O Divine Redeemer,"
"Bist du bei mir," "Jesu, Joy of
Man's Desiring," "Panus
Angelicus," "Ave Verum," and
more. (Philips 412629-2)
(BC: 28941-26292)

Beside Still Water. Medley of collection
of hymns (the "oldies") with pan
pipes. Volume 1 includes "When
Morning Gilds the Skies"; "It is
Well"; "Jesus Loves Me"; and
"Rock of Ages." (Brentwood CD
#5003) (ISBN: 55589-75187)
Volume 2 includes "What a Friend
We Have in Jesus"; "Blessed
Assurance"; and "How Firm a
Foundation." (ISBN: 55589-75179)

*The Gelineau Psalms—*The Choir of
the Cathedral Church of St. Mary,
Edinburgh. Based on the French
compositions of Joseph Gelineau
and translated into English as the
"Grail Version" of Psalms. (Example
given in Retreat Theme 1. Simple
Gifts, page 86.) Through G.I.A.
(CS-122)

*The Great Organ of the Washington
National Cathedral—*Douglas
Major, organist. Includes Bach's
"Toccata and Fugue in D Minor";
"Jesu, Joy of Man's Desiring";
"Sleepers, wake"; Suite from
Handel's "Water Music"; and others
by Franck, Purcell, Soler, King, and
a carillon sortie by Mulet. (Gothic:
49058) (BC: 00334-90582)

*Holy Radiant Light: The Sacred Song of
Russia—*Gloriae Dei Cantores.
Magnificent rendition of this music.
Paraclete Press, Orleans, MA.
Sacred music of the Orthodox
Church, including "Bogoroditse
Devo" (Rejoice, O Virgin) by
Rachmaninoff, Cherubic Hymn of
Glinka, and the familiar Otche Nash
(Our Father) by Kedrov.
(800/451-5006) (GDCD 007)
(BC: 09887-00072)

*Hymns Through the Centuries—*The
Cathedral Choral Society. This
album from the National Cathedral
includes familiar classic hymns with
organ, carillon, and peal bells. The
cassette or CD may be ordered by
calling the cathedral special choral
department number at
(202) 537–8980.

Hymns Triumphant I & II—London Philharmonic Choir and Orchestra. Forty-two hymns based on sequences of the Lord's Prayer. One piece leads into another. Cassette or CD (ISBN: 0061-66024 [I]; 0061-98171 [II])

Messe Solennelle de Sainte Cécile—Gounod. This version by the choir and orchestra of Radio France is listed as the top recording of this favorite. The "Sanctus" is the most familiar section, but all is an exquisite rendering the St. Cecilia Mass. (EMI: CDC 7470942)

Sacred Songs—Jessye Norman and the Ambrosian Singers. Features Gounod's "Sanctus," "The Holy City," "Amazing Grace," and "Let Us Break Bread Together." It also includes three Christmas songs and more. Philips. (400019-2) (BC: 28990-00192)

Voce—Choir of Trinity College, Cambridge, England. Includes an "Agnus Dei" sung to Samuel Barber's "Adagio for Strings" and Schubert's "Heilig" or "Sanctus." (Brentwood 5533J) (ISBN: 15589-79697; BC: 83061-55332)

Instrumental Music

Earth Songs—Narada Collection Series. Goes with the book "Earth Prayers." The pieces were inspired by selections from the book and the awareness that "we are, body and spirit, one with the Earth and with all of creation." (ND-63913) (BC: 83616-39132)

French Chamber Works for Harp—The Academy of St. Martin in the Fields Chamber Ensemble, with Skaila Kanga as harpist. Works featured are by Debussy, Ravel, Roussel. Especially delightful is the Fantasie for Violin and Harp, Op. 124, by Saint-Saens. Chandos Records: 8621; BC: 95115-86212.

Inner Peace—Steve Halpern. "Music for relaxation and well-being. Research has proven that this music helps you produce higher levels of alpha and theta brainwaves. These are the specific frequencies associated with meditation." (Sound RX 7850) (BC: 93791-78502)

Migration—Peter Kater (piano and synthesizers) and Carlos Nakai (Native-American flute, eagle bone, and chanting). These selections move in a pattern toward wholeness: "Wandering"—"Surrender"—"Embracing the Darkness"—"Transformation"—"Service," with many other phases in between. (SD704) (BC: 21585-07042)

Path of Joy. Extended version of "Jesu, Joy of Man's Desiring." Daniel Kobialka. Li-Sem Enterprises, 1775 Old County Rd., #9, Belmont, CA 94002 (Cassette: DK-103)

Sacred Sounds: Healing Music—Jorge Alfano. Alfano says that the use of music and sound as a tool for spiritual development can set us on a path to a better life. He refers to the Bible phrase, "In the beginning was the Word," or the soundless sound, which is vibration and energy. It is always expanding through the universe, creating other vibrations, each one denser and denser, heavier with each wave of expansion. All creation is an expression of that first vibration. Alfano is a master flutist who draws on different traditions to give meditation music. Accompanied by a booklet guide. The Relaxation Company, Inc. (CD 3186) (BC: 5229–63186–2)

The Sounds of Yosemite—The National Park Series. (A portion of the cost goes toward park maintenance.) Sounds of waterfalls, crickets, gentle rain, thunder, and streams recorded on location. An exquisite listening experience. Piano, acoustic guitar, violin, and keyboards. (Orange Tree Productions: OT 31111) (BC: 03503–11112)

Temple Garden—Bobu G. This is a favorite for the tranquility it brings and has been used for Tai Chi, meditation, and stress reduction. Played on the shakuhachi. Call 800/228–5711 (World Disc Productions)

Tibetan Bells II—Henry Wolff and Nancy Hennings. Using the magnificent bowl instruments of Tibetan origin, the composers present a space-poem in two sections, "Journey to the End," and "The Endless Journey" (about the progress of an individual soul or spirit as it proceeds through the last recognizable phases of existence. The resonances and duration of sound found in these bowls (also called bells) transport and surprise people. (Celestial Harmonies 13005–2) (BC: 1371–13005–2)

Timeless Motion. Extended version of Pachelbel's "Canon in D." Daniel Kobialka. Li-Sem Enterprises, 1775 Old County Rd., #9, Belmont, CA 94002 (Cassette: DK-102)

Velvet Dreams. Five extended versions by Kobialka. Pachelbel, "Canon in D"; Vivaldi, "Largo from Guitar Concerto"; Bach, "Sheep May Safely Graze"; Vivaldi, Largo from "Winter" of The Four Seasons; Bach, "Jesu, Joy of Man's Desiring." (CD: DK 305-2) (BC: 53221-73052)

Jazz

A Concert of Sacred Music from Grace Cathedral—Duke Ellington. The composer/performer said that he wrote this music in response to a growing understanding of his own vocation, and at the request of many clergy. He claims to be the messenger, bringing good news to people who have been raised in the church and do not take it seriously. Prestige Records. (BC: 01931–70018)

In This House, On This Morning—Wynton Marsalis. This began as a two-hour concert at the Lincoln Center, where the audience was given a panorama of human feeling rising through a form shaped in emulation of an Afro-American church service. The two CD volume includes a descriptive guide to the incredible presentation. (Columbia C2K 53220) (BC: 7464–53220–2)

The River—Monty Alexander. Piano, bass, and drums. A Jamaican Christian composes a jazz version of the hymn tunes and spirituals, as well as the original title tune. (Concord CD #CCD-4422)

Zoning—Mary Lou Williams. A Smithsonian/Folkways reissue. It is a collection of jazz, sensitively presented by the pianist and extremely suitable for meditation. Includes pieces with the titles "Gloria"; "Olinga" (also by Dizzy Gillespie); "Holy Ghost"; "Praise the Lord"; and "Syl-0-gism." CD 40811; BC: 9307-40811-2

Symphony

River Run—Stephen Albert. The four parts of this modern symphony, inspired by works of James Joyce, lend themselves to imagery and meditation. They are "Rain Music"; "Leafy Speafing"; "Beside the Rivering Waters"; and "RiversEnd." Mstislav Rostropovich, conductor, and the National Symphony Orchestra of Washington, DC. D/CD 1016; BC: 1349-11016-2

Symphony No. 3 in D Minor—Gustav Mahler. Recording by Leonard Bernstein. This work is especially moving in that it describes the composer's spiritual struggle as he presents a cosmological ascent culminating in a triumph both contemplative and explosive, proclaiming "Love God Alone All Your life." (2 CD set: Deutsche Grammophon #427328-2) (BC: 28942-73282)

Symphony No. 6 ("Pastoral")—Beethoven. This particular symphony was the result of the composer's delight in nature, despite the onset of his deafness. André Previn, conductor, and the Royal Philharmonic Orchestra. CD: 7747-2-RC; BC: 7863-57747-2

Taizé Music

Taizé Through bookstores/music stores/Cokesbury (800) 672-1789. *Laudate: Music of Taizé* (sung during evening prayer in Dublin, Ireland). Available on cassette and CD, although CD does not include "Ubi Caritas."

Taizé Through G.I.A. Publications, Inc., 7404 S. Mason Ave., Chicago, IL 60638. (800) 442-1358: *Alleluia* (CS-194); *Cantate* (CS-156) cassette only; *Songs and Prayers from Taizé* (CS-266); *Wait for the Lord* (CS-173); videocassette documentary *That Little Springtime* (30 min.), the story of Taizé, its life, song, and people. Songbooks are also available.

▍ Self-Nurture for Leaders

Edwards, Tilden. *Sabbath Time*. Nashville: Upper Room, 1992. A review of the concept of sabbath, its history, ways of observing it, and most of all the need to live it today.

Nouwen, Henri J. M. *In the Name of Jesus: Reflections on Christian Leadership*. New York: Crossroad, 1993. Guided by two passages of Scripture, the temptation of Jesus and Peter's call to feed sheep, Nouwen helps people deal with the temptations to be relevant, spectacular, and powerful in responding to "Do you love me?" "Feed my sheep," and "Somebody else will take you." He stresses the importance of contemplative prayer, confession and forgiveness, and theological reflection as a discipline. A small book with a powerful introduction and epilogue, it speaks to everyone in leadership positions.

Nouwen, Henri J. M. *The Way of the Heart: Desert Spirituality and Contemporary Ministry*. San Francisco: HarperSanFrancisco, 1991. Originally written as the result of a seminar at Yale Divinity School and subsequently presented as lectures, this little book speaks to the task and temptation of ministers today. Based on the seminar study of desert fathers and mothers, the essence is summed up in the following three chapter titles: solitude, silence, and prayer. It strikes home and motivates mightily.

Peterson, Eugene H. *Working the Angles: A Trigonometry for Pastoral Work*. Grand Rapids: Wm. B. Eerdmans Publishing Co., 1987. Here is a burning challenge for professionals: to not abandon one's calling by continuing to be a "shopkeeper"; but, pay attention! Specifically he urges more commitment to the spiritual practices of prayer, Scripture, and spiritual direction.

Sanford, John A. *Ministry Burnout*. Louisville, KY: Westminster/John Knox Press, 1992. A practical perception of expectations, needs, and problems encountered in ministry accompanied by references to the literature of myth, poem, and Scripture. A final chapter gives suggestions and images for finding renewing energy.

Westerhoff, John. *Spiritual Life: The Foundation for Preaching and Teaching*. Louisville, KY: Westminster/John Knox Press, 1994. Based on a course he taught at the College of Preachers (Washington National Cathedral), Westerhoff explores the special qualities needed for an informed spirituality and the ways to live it out, as well as offering suggestions for developing a personal discipline.

Spiritual Classics

Bobko, Jane (comp. and ed.). *Vision: The Life and Music of Hildegard of Bingen* (illus.). New York: Penguin Books, 1995. This is a beautifully illustrated introduction to the life, visions, and music of Hildegard of Bingen, an eleventh-century Benedictine mystic, who was also a prominent preacher, doctor, scientist, and artist.

Brother Lawrence (Robert J. Edmonson, trans.). *The Practice of the Presence of God*. Orleans, MA: Paraclete Press, 1985. Letters from a modest and unpretentious seventeenth-century monk, who happened to be lame and who experienced God's presence in the most ordinary of circumstances.

Durka, Gloria. *Praying with Julian of Norwich*. Winona, MN: St. Mary's Press, 1989. Selections from Julian's fourteenth-century writings are presented along with ways to reflect on the material in both a devotional and an informative style.

Fox, Matthew. *Meditations with Meister Eckhart* (illus.). Santa Fe, NM: Bear & Co., 1983. Meister Eckhart (1260–1329) was mystic and prophet, feminist and philosopher, preacher and theologian, administrator and poet, and a spiritual genius and declared heretic (for his prophetic preaching on behalf of the poor).

Hildegard of Bingen. *Hildegard of Bingen's Book of Divine Works with Letters and Songs*, edited by Matthew Fox. Santa Fe, NM: Bear & Co., 1987. Actual writings, not a commentary.

Hildegard of Bingen. *The Illuminations of Hildegard of Bingen*, edited by Matthew Fox (illus.). Santa Fe, NM: Bear & Co., 1985. Twenty-five full-page illuminations of this medieval mystic are presented with commentary from her writings. They represent her visions at the age of forty-two.

Johnston, William (trans.). *The Cloud of Unknowing*. New York: Image, 1996. A renowned mystical work written by an anonymous English monk in the fourteenth century.

Kelly, Thomas R. *A Testament of Devotion*. New York: HarperCollins, 1996. A small classic of devotional essays by a Quaker who sees the holy in the most common of places, in the most unexpected of events, and who addresses God in creative yet meaningful phrases.

Paulsell, William O. *Rules for Prayer*. Mahwah, NJ: Paulist Press, 1993. A book that draws on the greatest teachers and sources from the second century (i.e., the *Didache* and the *Rule of St. Benedict*) to modern guides such as Thomas Merton and Anthony Bloom. Divided into categories, according to style or intent, it proves most educational and engaging.

The Spiritual Exercises of St. Ignatius, translated by Anthony Mottola. New York: Image, 1964. Systematic meditations and prayers based on the life of Jesus.

St. John of the Cross. *Dark Night of the Soul*, translated and edited by E. Allison Peers. New York: Image, 1959. A Spanish mystic of the sixteenth century, a soulmate of St. Teresa of Avila, he writes about difficult experiences associated with dry periods in the spiritual life.

St. Teresa of Avila. *Interior Castle*, translated and edited by E. Allison Peers. New York: Image, 1961. Spanish mystic of the sixteenth century describes the soul's progress using the image of a castle and its mansions, just as the Gospel of John speaks of "many rooms."

Underhill, Evelyn. *Practical Mysticism*. Columbus: Ariel Press, 1986. This book is a smaller version of her classic tome *Mysticism*. Underhill was an English poet, novelist, and mystic who, while a lecturer at Oxford, led spiritual retreats as well as a prayer group of which she was the spiritual director.

Underhill, Evelyn. *The Spiritual Life*. Harrisburg, PA: Morehouse Publishing Co., 1984. A small gem of a book returned to print. See preceding entry for author information.

▌ Spiritual Fantasy

Borysenko, Joan and Joan Drescher. *On Wings of Light: Meditations for Awakening to the Source* (illus.). New York: Warner Books, 1992. This is an artistic book to encourage remembering what we already know. It also erases the illusion of separateness in creation. It is a call to wake up.

de Saint-Exupéry, Antoine. *The Little Prince*. New York: Harcourt Brace & Co., 1943. The classic tale that forever lends itself to rereading and sharing because of the profound wisdom always discovered within its pages.

Feldman, Christina and Jack Kornfield. *Soul Food: Stories to Nourish the Spirit and the Heart* (revised edition). New York: HarperSanFrancisco, 1996. A collection of stories—long and short, serious and humorous—from traditions across the globe.

Hays, Edward. *Sundancer: A Mystical Fantasy*. Leavenworth, KS: Forest of Peace Books, 1982. Magnificently written and illustrated allegory with abounding symbolism. For discussions about freedom, resurrection, self-worth, and holding fast to a dream.

Lehrman, Fredric, ed. *The Sacred Landscape*. Berkeley, CA: Celestial Arts, 1988. An exquisite collection of photographs around the earth coupled with brief descriptions and appropriate quotations. An artistic special that attracts coffee tables as well as the individual heart and eye.

Merrill, George R. and Robert J. Wicks. *Psychological and Spiritual Images of the Heart*. Mahwah, NJ: Paulist Press, 1990. A book to be experienced. Contains photographs that are accompanied by one or two sentences for contemplation and blank pages for writing down personal reflections. It is suggested in the brief guide that one focus on thoughts, feelings, images, and their effect on one's future behavior. A challenging way to meet God in the world.

Theophane the Monk. *Tales of a Magic Monastery*. New York: Crossroad, 1981. Through the medium of short stories or parables, new meanings are uncovered. Contains interesting illustrations.

▌Spiritual Growth

Artress, Lauren. *Walking a Sacred Path: Rediscovering the Labyrinth as a Spiritual Tool*. New York: Putnam, 1995. Using a model with a history of thousands of years, the author traces spiritual meanings and practices that have led to those of the present. The particular labyrinth with which the author works is found on the floor of Chartres Cathedral. Walking such a path can be more than symbolic of pilgrimage; it can be the essence of healing, spiritual insight, and awareness of the mind/body connection. The author also shares the dimensions of the labyrinth, encouraging others with her vision. A seed kit is available to those who wish to make one.

Cameron, Julia. *The Artist's Way: A Spiritual Path to Higher Creativity*. New York: Tarcher/Putnam, 1992. This is a splendid workbook for exploring one's creative gifts and linking them to spiritual insight and energy. The author assists the reader in being in touch with unrecognized blocks and leads the way into a holistic affirmation.

DelBene, Ron. *The Hunger of the Heart: A Call to Spiritual Growth*. Nashville: Upper Room, 1992. In a personal manner, the author responds to questions that arise in many circles today. He uses the image of a tree's growth to describe stages of spiritual development.

Ferguson, Duncan S., ed. *New Age Spirituality: An Assessment*. Louisville, KY: Westminster/John Knox Press, 1993. A variety of contributors, including Morton Kelsey, Harmon Bro, and Matthew Fox, give their views to help us discern the strengths and weaknesses found in new age approaches.

Foster, Richard. *Celebration of Discipline: The Path to Spiritual Growth*. New York: Harper & Row, 1988. A book that continues after twenty years to hold its own as a guide to the spiritual disciplines. Practices are divided into inward, outward, and corporate. A study guide is also available.

L'Engle, Madeleine. *Walking on Water: Reflections on Faith and Art*. Wheaton, IL: Shaw Publishers, 1980. A magnificent reflection on creativity and the opportunities we each have to live into our divine nudgings. The text is suitable for family discussion, with many examples of artists, great

and small, cited as they respond to the call. The author also poses tough questions for our day and humbly shares her own stories.

May, Gerald G. *Addiction and Grace* New York: Harper & Row, 1991. Drawing on his experiences as a psychiatrist working with the chemically dependent, May believes that addiction represents an attempt to assert complete control over our lives. He claims that such an attempt is doomed, and that only with God's help, by surrendering to grace, can we reach a harmonious resolution.

Mitchell, Stephen. *The Gospel According to Jesus: A New Translation and Guide to His Essential Teachings for Believers and Unbelievers*. New York: HarperCollins, 1993. Using a new translation from the Greek, the author has retained only the authentic sayings and doings of Jesus and omitted passages added by the early church. It is a very provocative and moving image of Jesus as a real person and a great spiritual teacher. The meditation is followed by a detailed and scholarly commentary.

Nouwen, Henri J. M. *The Way of the Heart: Desert Spirituality and Contemporary Ministry*. San Francisco: HarperSanFrancisco, 1991. Originally written as the outgrowth of a seminar at Yale Divinity School and subsequently presented as lectures, this little book speaks to the task and temptation of ministers today. Based on the seminar study of desert fathers and mothers, the essence is summed up in the three chapter titles: solitude, silence, and prayer. It strikes home and motivates mightily.

Palmer, Parker. *The Active Life: A Spirituality of Work, Creativity, and Caring*. San Francisco: Harper-SanFrancisco, 1992. An approach to the balance between spirituality and a life lived "in the world." A very useful book integrating contemplation with action and using stories and poems from Chang Tzu, Martin Buber, Jesus, and Esquivel.

Postema, Don. *Space for God: The Study and Practice of Prayer and Spirituality*. Grand Rapids: CRC Publications, 1983. A presentation of the spiritual life through reflections based on the Reformed tradition and incorporating art from Van Gogh and Rembrandt, as well as selected pieces of literature. Includes space for journal keeping. A leader's guide is also available.

Thompson, Marjorie. *Soul Feast: An Invitation to the Christian Spiritual Life*. Louisville, KY: Westminster John Knox Press, 1995. Henri Nouwen says in the introduction that this book, like few others, integrates a solid biblical vision and a practical hands-on approach to the spiritual life. Topics covered include spiritual reading, praying, worship, fasting, examination of conscience, spiritual guidance, hospitality, and the development of a "rule of life."

❙ Spiritual Guidance

Barry, William A. and William J. Connolly. *The Practice of Spiritual Direction*. San Francisco: HarperSanFrancisco, 1986. One of the earlier complete guides to spiritual direction, it covers relationships to God and to one another, as well as the matter of religious experience.

Dougherty, Rose Mary. *Group Spiritual Direction: Community for Discernment*. Mahwah, NJ: Paulist Press, 1995. Unlike the one-to-one relationship that might first come to mind, this form of guidance addresses a group of people who choose to listen attentively to one another and God's Spirit. The author covers questions, definitions, process, and relationships in an easy, conversational style.

Dyckman, K. M. and L. P. Carroll. *Inviting the Mystic, Supporting the Prophet: An Introduction to Spiritual Direction*. Mahwah, NJ: Paulist Press, 1981. This book is written to encourage lay people and clergy to confidently use their gifts to become spiritual directors to others. Topics include a definition of spiritual direction, presuppositions about the director and about prayer, praying through the desert, prayerful decision making, and mystics and prophets.

Edwards, Tilden. *Spiritual Friend: Reclaiming the Gift of Spiritual Direction*. New York: Paulist Press, 1980. A guide to learning about the background of spiritual direction, as well as the practical aspects of seeking or being a spiritual friend. A good introduction to the subject.

Farnham, Suzanne, et al. *Listening Hearts: Discerning Call in Community*. Harrisburg, PA: Morehouse Publishing Co., 1993. This is the story of a group in the Baltimore area who met to wrestle with the issues of call, discernment, and community. "Does God call ordinary people? And if so, to what? How can we distinguish God's voice from all of the other voices that clamor at us? How can we find support for our calls? And how can we remain faithful and accountable to them?" A provocative study with suggestions, an outstanding appendix, and annotated bibliography. Also available are a leader's manual, a songbook, and a book of retreat designs with meditation exercises and leader's guidelines.

Fischer, Kathleen. *Women at the Well: Feminist Perspectives on Spiritual Direction*. Mahwah, NJ: Paulist Press, 1988. A creative book on working with women in spiritual direction that is scholarly, personal (with stories), and helpful (concrete suggestions for prayer and reflection).

Gratton, Carolyn. *The Art of Spiritual Guidance*. New York: Crossroad, 1993. Covers the importance of freedom and wholeness, the entrance into mystery, and being realistic about life's circumstances. This is a valuable reference and guide, especially as it encourages the director to be open, honest, and willing to love.

Guenther, Margaret. *Holy Listening: The Art of Spiritual Direction*. Boston: Cowley Press, 1992. A very warm account of what happens when we meet one another as strangers. Stressing the importance of hospitality over the need to be right (by either party), the author brings personal tidbits of her experience into a delightful and instructive book. Parts of the book are intended to be especially helpful to women.

Hart, Thomas. *The Art of Christian Listening*. New York: Paulist Press, 1980. An excellent beginning book on the subject, it is concise, to the point, describes what spiritual direction is and what it is not. In each chapter there are reflection and discussion questions, as well as suggestions for further reading.

Kelsey, Morton T. *Companions on the Inner Way: The Art of Spiritual Guidance*. New York: Crossroad, 1995. This text on spiritual direction covers the traditions of Christianity, as well as the kinds of beliefs, religious experiences, and psychological implications for engaging in this practice.

Leech, Kenneth. *Soul Friend: The Practice of Christian Spirituality*. New York: Harper & Row, 1980. One of the earlier modern-day classics in this field. Emphasis is given to historical background for the practice, the nature of spirituality and prayer practice, and the difference between direction, counseling, and therapy. A good introduction to the subject.

May, Gerald G. *Care of Mind, Care of Spirit: A Psychiatrist Explores Spiritual Direction*. San Francisco: HarperSanFrancisco, 1992. Written to help spiritual directors appreciate the psychospiritual aspects of individuals, this book also provides sound information on the heritage of spiritual direction and the human being's longing for—and resistance to—God.

Nemeck, F. K. and M. T. Coombs. *The Way of Spiritual Direction*. Collegeville, MN: Liturgical Press, 1985. An extraordinarily complete review of spiritual direction principles, relationships, difficulties, and hopes.

Yungblut, John R. *The Gentle Art of Spiritual Guidance*. New York: Continuum, 1995. A bit different from the usual guide, this one is based on the author's strong devotion to Teilhard de Chardin's creation spirituality and to Jungian psychology. It has been used by The Guild for Spiritual Guidance in Rye, New York, where the Quaker author taught for a number of years.

Spirituality and Children

Berends, Polly Berrien. *Gently Lead: How to Teach Your Children About God While Finding Out for Yourself*. New York: HarperPerennial, 1992 . A book full of stories, poems, thoughts, and meditations, along with some parental guidelines for introducing spirituality to children.

O'Callaghan Scheiling, Theresa and Louis M. Savary. *Our Treasured Heritage: Teaching Christian Meditation to Children*. New York: Crossroad, 1981. Specific meditations for the church year. Introduces children to meditation and centering. Gives practical how-to steps and provides meditations through the liturgical year.

Coles, Robert. *The Spiritual Life of Children*. New York: Houghton Mifflin, 1991. On the basis of time spent with children, the author conveys the depth of thought and feeling in their interviews with him, in their drawings and paintings, and in their disputations among themselves. Topics include the nature of God's wishes, the devil, heaven and hell, and faith and skepticism.

▌ The Use of Story

Bender, Sue. *Plain and Simple: A Woman's Journey to the Amish*. San Francisco: HarperCollins, 1989. This books lends itself to an examination of our priorities in life, how we were raised to view life, and the challenge to see things through a different lens.

Brooke, Avery. *Finding God in the World: Reflections on a Spiritual Journey*. Boston: Cowley Press, 1994. A personal journal of experiences in life that center around the author's spiritual journey. It encourages others to see that God works through story, humor, and real—sometimes unbelievable—circumstances.

Bunyan, John. *Pilgrim's Progress*. Classic found in many editions. Next to the Bible, this book is thought to have been the most widely read piece of literature. It is also ranked by most literary critics as the greatest allegory in any language. It can be used personally or in groups to examine the various stages of spiritual growth. It also provides opportunity for Jungian study of archetypes.

Fynn. *Mister God, This is Anna*. New York: Ballantine Books, 1985. Looking and listening to children's experiences and insights, the author leads one to a sense of openness to that childlike faith.

Kidd, Sue Monk. *When the Heart Waits: Spiritual Direction for Life's Sacred Questions*. San Francisco: HarperCollins, 1990. The author's personal story of struggles and challenges to new places of spiritual growth that involved long periods of waiting. Includes references to a vast number of spiritual giants.

L'Engle, Madeleine. *A Circle of Quiet* (San Francisco: HarperSanFrancisco, 1977); *The Irrational Season* (San Francisco: HarperSanFrancisco, 1983); and *The Summer of the Great-Grandmother* (San Francisco: HarperSanFrancisco, 1980). In these books, the author willingly shares personal experiences and insights, much of which is spiritual wisdom for today. See also *Walking on Water: Reflections on Faith and Art*. Wheaton, IL: Shaw Publishers, 1980.

May, Gerald G. *The Awakened Heart*. San Francisco: HarperSanFrancisco, 1991. Although this is not a "story" per se, it arises out of the author's own story. It enables the reader to accompany the author in practicing the presence of love.

Weems, Ann. *Family Faith Stories*. Louisville, KY: Westminster/John Knox Press, 1989. Reflections on the author's family and her religious heritage through anecdotal stories and poems. A way to invite others to tell their stories.

Wiederkehr, Macrina. *A Tree Full of Angels: Seeing the Holy in the Ordinary*. New York: Harper & Row, 1990. Wiederkehr's story invites us to stop and see the simple things of life. A collection of quotations from literature and Scripture are mixed with her personal and inviting reflections. Also included are some of her poems, which delight with their creative images.

Appendixes

Appendix
A

▌ Public Relations Samples

This appendix includes publicity samples that succeeded in:

1. Identifying a target group who should receive personal invitations by letter
2. Producing an attractive flier that is easy to read, has essential information, and has a registration form
3. Producing bookmarks for promotional/registration tables—as a take-home reminder
4. Using the same logo on multiple forms of publicity so it can be recognized and associated with the event
5. Inserting a half-sheet information page with retreat logo in the church bulletin
6. Providing information about the leader(s)
7. Soliciting quotations from the leader(s) for inclusion and stimulation.

Invitation

(Date)

(Name)
(Address)

Dear Friends:

We wanted to send a special note to you, along with the enclosed flyer, about the "Silent Retreat" which is scheduled for *(dates)*. Our retreat leader has excellent credentials and experience.

There are a limited number of spaces available, and thus, if you are interested in this kind of retreat we encourage you to sign up early.

If you have further questions, please give me a call.

Sincerely,

(Name), Chairperson
Planning Committee
(Name), Staff to Planning Committee

Enclosure

Flyer—Front

Clergy and Educators

Treat Yourself to a

Special Retreat

(*Dates*)

(*Time*)

at
(*Location*)

Theme:
(*Topic*)

Leader:
(*Name*)

Flyer—Reverse

The Planning Committee is pleased to offer you an opportunity to breathe in the glories of nature in sound and silence, along with the Word.

Facilities: (*Give description*)

Cost: $ (*Fee and whether it includes meals or room and board*)

Because of the limitation of available space, reservations will be taken on a "first come, first served" basis.

Outline of Schedule:
(*see sample below*)

Noon—Arrival and lunch
Introductions and first presentation
Quiet time
Dinner
Second presentation
Quiet time
Vespers

Morning prayer
Breakfast
Third presentation
Quiet time
Closing worship

Retreat Leader:
(*Name and list of qualifications*)

Registration

Name: _____

Address: _____

_____

Phone (Home): _____

(Work): _____

In order to hold your place, please enclose a check for _____ , payable to _____ Presbytery and note "Retreat" in the lower left corner.

Thanks.

Bookmark

Women's Retreat

(Date of retreat)

*Simple Gifts . . .
Nurturing
Our Desire
for God*

*O God,
you are my God,
earnestly
I seek you.
(Ps. 63:1)*

Women's Retreat

(Date of retreat)

*Simple Gifts . . .
Nurturing
Our Desire
for God*

*O God,
you are my God,
earnestly
I seek you.
(Ps. 63:1)*

Women's Retreat

(Date of retreat)

*Simple Gifts . . .
Nurturing
Our Desire
for God*

*O God,
you are my God,
earnestly
I seek you.
(Ps. 63:1)*

Half-page Bulletin Insert

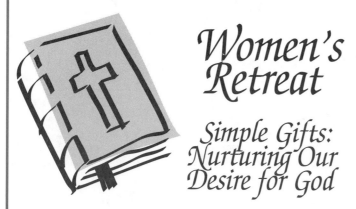

Women's Retreat

Simple Gifts: Nurturing Our Desire for God

(*Date*)

at

(*Location*)

Many of us find that we yearn for closer communion with God, especially during these times. (*Name of retreat leader*), our gifted retreat leader, intuitively guides individuals and groups to a deeper relationship with God. "Simple gifts" of praying the Psalms, praying to "slow down," and putting ourselves into the stories of Scripture will enable us to listen for the quiet voice of God. Come and be refreshed!

The retreat cost of $_____ includes:

_____.

Child care (*what is offered*)

Scholarships are available. Please call (*name*) at (*phone number*) for details.

To register, call (*name*) at (*phone number*) or drop by the Registration Table in (*location*) after each service on (*dates*). Registration deadline is (*date*).

Women's Retreat

Simple Gifts: Nurturing Our Desire for God

(*Date*)

at

(*Location*)

Many of us find that we yearn for closer communion with God, especially during these times. (*Name of retreat leader*), our gifted retreat leader, intuitively guides individuals and groups to a deeper relationship with God. "Simple gifts" of praying the Psalms, praying to "slow down," and putting ourselves into the stories of Scripture will enable us to listen for the quiet voice of God. Come and be refreshed!

The retreat cost of $_____ includes:

_____.

Child care (*what is offered*)

Scholarships are available. Please call (*name*) at (*phone number*) for details.

To register, call (*name*) at (*phone number*) or drop by the Registration Table in (*location*) after each service on (*dates*). Registration deadline is (*date*).

Appendix

B

❚ Journal Covers and Ideas

The first assumption is that journals will be provided. Whether or not people use them for journaling is not important. Providing a journal booklet gives the participant a way to record any notes, impressions, and responses that might be called for. It is also interesting to note that people tend to keep these "souvenirs" of the event since they record feelings and expressions of faith or desire for God.

Samples included here have been used for congregational retreats, prayer workshops, officers' retreats, judicatory silent retreats, church school teacher events, and retreats for ministerial candidates.

Cover designs may be original or may be adapted from other materials. If you use original artwork, be sure to secure permission from the artist or the publisher and include this credit information in the book.

Journal Cover

Nurturing

Our Spiritual Roots

Journal Covers

"Give me a drink." (John 4:7)

▍ Journaling Ideas

For those who have discovered the value of using a journal, whether it be a spiral drugstore notebook or a lovely bound edition with blank pages, there is the realization that we often write about our innermost feelings, gaining access to hidden depths of our being. We often repress more than we care to admit, and journaling sometimes helps to surface those things that God would have us deal with for our personal growth. The following are ideas for journaling.

1. Begin "Dear God" and write about all that is going on in your life, especially including your feelings.

2. Take a Scripture passage where Jesus is talking with someone. Be that person and dialogue with Jesus. For example, Bar-timaeus (son of Timaeus or Bat-timaeus (daughter of Timaeus).

Jesus: What do you want me to do for you?
Your name: (*whatever comes*)
Jesus: (*whatever seems to want to be written*)

Go back and forth in writing this dialogue until you come to some sense of closure.

3. What are the things that *assist* your attentiveness to God? What are the things that *hinder* your attentiveness and get you "off track"?

4. Write a prayer of your "soul's sincere desire."

5. Write a poem or story.

6. Respond to how God seems to be calling you right now. To what place in your journey?

7. Make a list of questions that you would like to ask God or Jesus. Ponder them in silence for a few minutes and then write anything that seems to have been imagined, intuited, or made clearer. If there is nothing, then simply give thanks for the silent communion in a written prayer.

8. Write your personal confession. Consider taking it to someone whom you consider to be a spiritual friend.

9. How does it seem that God is dealing with you these days? What does that movement look like?

10. Write a psalm of thanksgiving or lament.

11. *Write your own ideas below.*

Appendix

C

∎ Sample Evaluation Forms

This appendix contains forms that have been used for various kinds of events. The form that is used will usually depend on the expectations of the leader, or the leadership team. The word *feedback* tends to be a more friendly term.

Evaluation A (General)

1. Did this time together meet your expectations? If so, how?

2. What was the "high" point of the retreat for you or what spoke to you?

3. What was the least helpful part of the retreat or what would you have changed?

Evaluation B (for a six-week session)

Please complete the following and turn in before leaving.

1. What has been most helpful in terms of

   Content?

   Process?

   Leadership?

2. Do you think anything could have been done differently?

3. If you were to summarize the benefits of this six-week series (or other event) for you personally—in a word or a phrase—what might that be?

4. Was there anything that was especially meaningful that might influence you in the way you are present for God?

5. Do you have any other feedback for the leaders in terms of their assisting or impeding your direct presence for God?

Summary of the six sessions:

(A description of the scripture/theme is given for each week to aid participants' recollection.)

Evaluation C (for a retreat)

1. Did this time together meet your expectations?

2. What was the high point for you?

3. What was the low point?

4. What would you do differently? (add, eliminate, substitute, change)

5. Please indicate how helpful or nurturing you felt each retreat activity was *for you* by using the following rating system:

   3= *excellent*   2= *good*   1= *just that*   0= *not helpful at all*

   ___ Get-acquainted time
   ___ *The Way of the Heart* presentation and reflection
   ___ Panel
   ___ Vespers
   ___ Fun and Fellowship
   ___ Morning Prayer
   ___ Round Robin Options
   ___ Time for One-on-One
   ___ Role-playing stories
   ___ Closing Worship/Communion

6. Do you have any other suggestions?

Evaluation D (for a Lenten series or similar event)

1. Each of the sessions had similar components. Please circle the number that most closely parallels the value that each part had for you.

	Least → Most				
Total group sharing	1	2	3	4	5
Content	1	2	3	4	5
Experience of meditation, chant, singing, Scripture	1	2	3	4	5
Silence	1	2	3	4	5
journaling	1	2	3	4	5
Small group sharing	1	2	3	4	5

2. Was there any session or experience that was particularly difficult for you to become involved in?

3. Was there a highlight that you would want to cite?

4. Did this series help you with your relationship with God?

5. What are the strengths of this series? Please list below.

6. Do you have any suggestions for the leader? Are there any areas that the leader needs to work on?

Evaluation E (General)

1. Was this a positive experience for you? (*Check one.*)

___ Very much
___ Yes
___ So so
___ Not really

2. What one or two things will you carry with you from this experience?

3. What was the most helpful part of the retreat/event/workshop for you? the least helpful?

4. Do you have any suggestions/comments?

Endnotes

Chapter 5

1. This was heard by the pilot group for Group Leaders Program, which is sponsored by the Shalem Institute for Spiritual Formation. For more information, write to the following address: 5430 Grosvenor Lane, Bethesda, MD 20814; or call (301) 897-7334; fax (301) 897-3719.
2. Anthony de Mello, *Awareness: A De Mello Spirituality Conference in His Own Words*. Edited by J. Francis Stroud. Copyright © 1990 by the Center for Spiritual Exchange (New York: Doubleday, 1990).

Chapter 6

1. Daniel Kobialka, *Path of Joy*. To order, write Li-Sem Enterprises, 1775 Old County Road, #9, Belmont, CA 94002.
2. From *The Way of the Heart,* by Henri J. M. Nouwen, pp. 37–38. Copyright © 1981 by Henri J. M. Nouwen. (New York: HarperCollins Publishers, Inc., 1986). Used by permission.
3. Ibid.

Chapter 7

1. For more information on the Shalem Institute for Spiritual Formation, write to the following address: 5430 Grosvenor Lane, Bethesda, MD 20814; or call (301) 897-7334; fax (301) 897-3719.
2. For more complete descriptions of some of these practices, see *Living in the Presence: Disciplines for the Spiritual Heart*, by Tilden H. Edwards, Jr., Executive Director of Shalem Institute for Spiritual Formation (San Francisco: HarperSanFrancisco, 1987), pp. 132–140.
3. From *Sadhana—A Way to God: Christian Exercises in Eastern Form*, by Anthony de Mello, pp. 7–8. Copyright © 1978 by Anthony de Mello, S.J. Used by permission of Doubleday, a division of Bantam Doubleday Dell Publishing Group, Inc.
4. Taken from notes of Tilden Edwards' presentation in a Shalem program given on November 12, 1984.
5. *The Psalms: An Inclusive Language Version Based on the Grail Translation from the Hebrew.* Copyright © 1963, 1986 Ladies of the Grail (England).
6. From *The Psalms: A New Translation for Prayer and Worship*, translated by Gary Chamberlain. Copyright © 1984 by The Upper Room.
7. Leslie F. Brandt, *Psalms/Now* (St. Louis: Concordia Publishing House, 1973).
8. John Michael Talbot, *Come to the Quiet* (Canoga Park, CA: Sparrow Records, 1980). To order, write to Sparrow Records, 8025 Deering Ave., Canoga Park, CA 91304.
9. *The Gelineau Psalms*, translated and arranged by Joseph Gelineau; sung by the Choir of The Cathedral Church of St. Mary, Edinburgh. Chicago: G.I.A. Publications, Inc. To order, write to G.I.A. Publications, Inc., 7404 S. Mason Ave., Chicago, IL 60638.
10. I was introduced to this idea by Eileen Colbert on November 19, 1984, at a long-term Shalem group.
11. *The Philokalia*, translated and edited by G. E. H. Palmer, Philip Sherrard, and Kallistos Ware, vol. 1. Copyright © 1979 by The Eling Trust (London: Faber & Faber, 1979).

12. *The Way of a Pilgrim*, translated by R. M. French. Copyright © 1965 by Mrs. Eleanor French. Copyright renewed.

13. Ira Progoff, *The Practice of Process Meditation* (New York: Dialogue House Library, 1980), pp. 187–193.

14. John H. Westerhoff, *Inner Growth, Outer Change* (New York: Seabury Press, 1979), p. 133.

15. Per-Olof Sjögren, *The Jesus Prayer* (Philadelphia: Fortress Press, 1975).

16. *The Way of a Pilgrim,* p. 41.

17. Ibid., p. 10.

18. From a presentation by Tilden Edwards, November 26, 1984, as part of a Shalem long-term introductory program.

19. *Laudate*, Music of Taizé. Music by Jacques Berthier. To order, please contact Cokesbury.

20. Ibid.

21. John Welch, *Spiritual Pilgrims: Carl Jung and Teresa of Avila*, p. 65. Copyright © 1982 by John Welch, O.Carm (New York: Paulist Press, 1982). Used by permission.

22. Ibid., p. 61

23. Excerpted from *With Open Hands*, by Henri J. M. Nouwen, pp. 2–3. Copyright © 1995 by Ave Maria Press, Notre Dame, IN 46556. Used with permission of the publisher.

24. Adapted from *Celtic Meditations: Moments of Thanksgiving, Invitations to Eucharist,* by Edward J. Farrell, pp. 106–108. Copyright © 1976, published by Dimension Books, Inc., Denville NJ 07834.

25. From *The Edge of Glory*, by David Adams, p. 51. Copyright © 1985 by David Adams. Reprinted by permission of Morehouse Publishing.

26. Parts of this section are from Tilden Edwards' session on October 29, 1984, in Shalem's long-term prayer group. These sessions were incorporated in his book *Living in the Presence: Disciplines for the Spiritual Heart* (San Francisco: HarperSanFrancisco, 1987), ch. 3.

27. Tibetan bells were introduced to me by Elise Wiarda, a graduate of Shalem's Spiritual Guidance Program and a spiritual director and massage therapist. I found the prolonged sound to be an incredible aid to interior stillness and subsequently sought my own.

28. Used at a Shalem group presentation, November 27, 1985, by the Rev. Carole A. Crumley, Shalem Associate Staff Member and former Canon Educator at the Washington National Cathedral.

29. Julian of Norwich, *Showings*, translated by Edmund E. Colledge and James Walsh. Copyright © 1978 by The Missionary Society of St. Paul the Apostle in the State of New York (New York: Paulist Press, 1978).

30. Ibid., p. 183.

▌Chapter 8

1. Anne Shotwell is a member of Vienna Presbyterian Church, Vienna, Virginia, who writes poetry for herself, others, and special events. She also publishes a monthly inspirational booklet sent out as "*Gleanings from Anne's Own Garden—or personal reflection or family sharing.*" Each month is devoted to a special theme and includes reflection questions. She can be reached at 2721 Valestra Circle, Oakton, VA 22124.

2. Daniel Kobialka, *Path of Joy.* To order, write Li-Sem Enterprises, 1775 Old County Road, #9, Belmont, CA 94002.

3. "Morning Has Broken," from Tommy Reilly and Skaila Kanga, *British Folksongs* (Ocean, NJ: Musical Heritage Society, Inc., 1990). Arranged for Harmonica and Harp. Compact Disc #MHS 512596A

4. From *The Psalms: A New Translation for Prayer and Worship*, translated by Gary Chamberlain. Copyright © 1984 by The Upper Room.

5. With thanks to Vienna Presbyterian Church, Vienna, Virginia.

6. Ann Belford Ulanov, *Picturing God* (Boston: Cowley Publications, 1986).

7. Virginia R. Mollenkott, *The Divine Feminine: The Biblical Imagery of God as Female* (New York: Crossroad, 1985).

8. Thomas R. Hawkins, *The Potter and the Clay: Meditations on Spiritual Growth* (Nashville: The Upper Room, 1986).

9. Fynn, *Mister God, This Is Anna* (New York: Ballantine Books, 1976).

10. Alice Walker, *The Color Purple* (New York: Washington Square Press, 1982).

11. Ulanov, *Picturing God.*

12. Nelle Morton, *The Journey Is Home* [Louisville, KY: Presbyterian Church (U.S.A.), 1989]; book by the same title (Boston: Beacon Press, 1985).

13. From *Wholeness in Worship*, by Thomas N. Emswiler, p. 102. Copyright © 1980 by Thomas Neufer Emswiler and Sharon Neufer Emswiler (New York: HarperCollins, 1980).

14. "God Be in My Head," *The Pilgrim Hymnal* (New York: Pilgrim Press, 1985), no. 543.

15. From *Encounters with Silence*, by Karl Rahner, p. 6. Reprinted with the permission of the publisher. Copyright © 1960 by Karl Rahner. Published by Christian Classics, A Division of RCL • Resources for Christian Living, 200 East Bethany Drive, Allen, TX 75002.

16. Used by permission of Rev. George L. Miller, D Min., as quoted in *alive now!* Nov/Dec 1987, p. 16.

17. Sue Bender, *Plain and Simple: A Woman's Journey to the Amish* (San Francisco: HarperCollins, 1989).

18. Tilden H. Edwards, *Spiritual Friend: Reclaiming the Gift of Spiritual Direction* (New York: Paulist Press, 1980).

19. Rose Mary Dougherty, S.S.N.D., *Group Spiritual Direction: Community for Discernment* (Mahwah, NJ: Paulist Press, 1995).

20. From *The Active Life: A Spirituality of Work, Creativity, and Caring*, by Parker J. Palmer. Copyright © 1990 by Parker J. Palmer. HarperCollins Publishers, Inc.

21. I am indebted to Sidney Skirvin, pastor of Church of the Pilgrims, Washington, DC, for his use of this chapter at a clergy-educator retreat on discernment in 1991.

22. Palmer, *The Active Life*, p. 66. Used by permission.

23. The Dameans, *Intermissions: Song-Meditations for Personal and Communal Prayer* (South Weymouth: Damean Music, 1988). Can be obtained from G.I.A. Publications, Inc. (800) GIA-1358

24. *The Collected Works of St. John of the Cross*, translated by Kieran Kavanaugh and Otilio Rodriguez (Washington, DC: Institute of Carmelite Studies Publications, 1979).

25. H. Richard Niebuhr as cited at a retreat led by Pastor Sidney Skirvin, Church of the Pilgrims, Washington, DC, 1991.

26. "Abba Father," album *Earthen Vessels*, St. Louis Jesuits and New Dawn Music, 1973. OCP, 5536 NE Hassalo, Portland, OR 97213. (Cassette: 9465; Compact Disc: 9464)

27. Ibid.

28. Paul Winter, *Missa Gaia /Earth Mass* (Compact Disc #LD0002, Litchfield, CT: Living Music).

29. Veronica Zundel, ed. *Eerdman's Book of Famous Prayers: A Treasury of Christian Prayers through the Centuries*. Copyright © 1983 by Lion Publishing (Grand Rapids: Wm. B. Eerdmans Publishing Co., 1984), p. 43.

30. Gloria Durka, *Praying with Julian of Norwich* (Winona, MN: St. Mary's Press, 1989).
31. Anthony de Mello, *Sadhana: A Way to God* (New York: Doubleday, 1978), pp. 81–82.